The Mastery of Customer Service
in Careers

The Mastery of Customer Service in Careers

J. Mark Munoz, Nigel Hill, and Diane M. Crutcher

BEP

BUSINESS EXPERT PRESS

Leader in applied, concise business books

The Mastery of Customer Service in Careers

First published in 2025 by
Business Expert Press, LLC
222 East 46th Street, New York, NY 10017
www.businessexpertpress.com

ISBN-13: 978-1-63742-808-5 (paperback)
ISBN-13: 978-1-63742-809-2 (e-book)

Business Expert Press Business Career Development Collection

First edition: 2025

10 9 8 7 6 5 4 3 2 1

EU SAFETY REPRESENTATIVE

Mare Nostrum Group B.V.
Mauritskade 21D
1091 GC Amsterdam
The Netherlands
gpsr@mare-nostrum.co.uk

Description

The Mastery of Customer Service in Careers highlights the experiences of three high school buddies who reached the pinnacle of their careers in service.

The three men—a general, a medical doctor who founded a successful chain of wellness clinics, and a professor who serves as director of a global hotel business—recount the career challenges they faced and their pathways to success. Along with a highly accomplished daughter of one of the men, they provide insights to two young adults looking to embark on careers grounded in customer satisfaction.

This book is exceptionally valuable to all those executives worldwide who wish to elevate their performance in customer service. Using an easy to read, relatable, and engaging story as a backdrop, the book underscores the essential elements of service excellence. Each chapter includes an academically grounded and practice-oriented discussion that provides readers with the foundation for providing unparalleled and impactful service within an organization and in our society.

Contents

Testimonials

"The storytelling style of this book makes for an easy and entertaining read. The Mastering Customer Service sections drive home key ideas presented in each chapter. Having spent my entire professional career in customer service, I thoroughly enjoyed reading this book and would highly recommend it to anyone whether new to the industry or one with vast knowledge of customer service. **The Mastery of Customer Service in Careers** *is a must read!"*
—**Wes Tindal, COO, National Customer Service Association**

*"***The Mastery of Customer Service in Careers** *is a must read! This book offers powerful insights and actionable strategies that will help executives stand out from the competition. It's an essential guide for anyone looking to take service performance to new heights and lead in their industry."*—**Reginald J. Baron, Director, Mobile Sales/Field Security Operations, Revenue Control. MTA New York City Transit**

"All the king's horses and all the king's men cannot make your customers come back to you again. Businesses spend so much money to attract new customers and then forget to serve them well. I really like how this book focuses on what it means to deliver a 'professional' customer service experience and what that can do to have your people loving your brand. "—**Brian Johnson, CEO and Cofounder of Katapult Network**

Prologue

The Mastery of Customer Service in Careers is a story about three gentlemen who were invited to spend a summer vacation with one of their daughters and her family in their large summer home in South Carolina.

The gentlemen were high school friends who have all recently retired. In their own way, they have each reached the pinnacle of a professional career in service. With time on their hands, they decided to join the family in their summer home to do some fishing, catch up, reminisce the good old days, and deliberate on their future.

The family consisting of a mother and her career-bound twins welcomes the highly accomplished gentlemen to join them in their summer adventure as they celebrate college graduation and consider upcoming life and career choices.

During the course of the trip, the gentlemen share their life and career lessons with the family. They offer them the best of their collective wisdom on ways to find exceptional and enduring success in the world of service, acknowledging having learned from their own growth opportunities and so many phenomenal role models along the way.

In the story of their time together, you will encounter an entrepreneurial medical doctor who cofounded a national health and wellness retail chain, an internationally renowned business professor who also serves on the board of a globally recognized hotel chain, and a U.S. Army General who led many successful military operations throughout his career. As they enter the twilight stage of their lives, the gentlemen draw upon their past experiences to offer advice to the family facing important life decisions: a mother contemplating a change in career, a daughter considering a service career, and a son hoping to find success in customer service in the corporate world.

In writing this book, we authors pondered our lives of service in a variety of professions, including higher education, health care, and marketing. We are established authors, professionals, consultants, business owners, and entrepreneurs. As we contemplated our life's work, one word consistently stood out—service. Almost every working day in our lives was about service—serving families, colleagues, organizations, students, readers, clients, patients and our communities.

In thinking back on our service careers, we realized that there isn't much literature or stories that emphasize the **power of service**, and this book is intended to begin to fill that gap. The story is designed to be simple, engaging, and filled with practical insights drawn from research and personal experiences.

Each chapter starts with a story and concludes with an executive overview titled "Mastering Customer Service." The overview offers innovative ideas and methodologies to help readers attain the highest levels of service and customer satisfaction.

We hope that the story and shared ideas will inspire you to live a life of exceptional commitment to serve others and motivate you to pursue the highest level of service be it in a personal, professional, or business capacity. Enjoy this book of "insights" and let it be a guide in your pursuit of service excellence!

J. Mark Munoz, Nigel Hill, Diane M. Crutcher

CHAPTER 1

Help Others

Life's most persistent and urgent question is: what are you doing for others?

—Martin Luther King, Jr., American Minister

Ray Richardson peeked outside from the window of his house. Then, his cell phone rang.

"Hello" he said enthusiastically,

Glenn? How are you? Great! You'll be here in about 30 minutes you said? I look forward to meeting Liza and your grandkids. It's so nice of Liza to invite us to her summer home in South Carolina. I'm all set. This will be fun and hopefully the fishing will be great too. Okay, see you soon.

By force of habit, he looked at his watch. It was 9:00 a.m., and he knew his two old friends were very particular about the use of time, having lived very busy schedules throughout their lives.

Then a realization dawned upon him, "Darn," he thought, "I'm retired now, and my buddies have just recently retired too. Who cares about time? What's the rush?"

He sat on his sofa and started reminiscing. This summer marked the 50th year of their high school graduation. To celebrate, he and his friends decided to go on a fishing trip and spend their summer as guests in the home of one of their daughters. He was looking forward to seeing Glenn Thompson again. It would be nice to meet and get to know Glenn's daughter Liza and his grandkids. Was it 30 years since he last saw him? His other good friend, Sergio Martinez, was also joining them. The three of them were inseparable during their high school days. They were active members of the Amnesty International Club and were passionate about campaigning for human rights around the world. On several evenings during high school, they had talked about their life ambitions, challenges, and even love interests.

What a long and amazing journey he had since high school! What were the odds that as an average African American student from a poor family, he would end up getting into a premier medical school and graduating near the top of his class. Equally surprising is that his specialization in longevity medicine would be of very high demand and that, aside from a successful practice, he ended up cofounding a large national retail chain focusing on health and wellness. He retired last year but opted to stay as a member of the Board to continue to help advance the health of seniors and the immunocompromised. Few in his high school class would have predicted his success.

His friends Sergio and Glenn, on the other hand, would never have doubted his abilities. Throughout the years, they had all stayed in touch and been a constant source of support and inspiration for one another. In his view, it was their mutual passion to help others that supported each of them in reaching the pinnacle of their professions.

Sergio Martinez worked his way through college as a salesman for an agricultural supply company. He eventually got an MBA from a top-tier university and then a PhD in Management. He pursued his career in academia and achieved the highest academic rank of full professor at an established university receiving multiple international teaching and research awards and being globally recognized for his publications on customer service. He retired a couple of years ago but continues to serve as a board member for an international hotel chain. As a second-generation Latin American from a poor family, he had done very well for himself.

Glenn Thompson was a total surprise. After high school, Ray thought that Glenn would pursue a degree in engineering. He was great at mechanical work, no doubt inherited from his father, who had a small car repair business. Given that the three of them came from poor families, none of them could afford a car. They collaborated as a team and got car scrap parts from a junkyard. Glenn took the lead and assembled the car from scratch. The car ended up as a functional vehicle that paved the way for the three of them to go around town, on dates, and even take occasional camping trips.

Ray imagined that with his skills, Glenn would make a great engineer. Glenn, however, took an entirely different path. He joined the U.S. Army after graduation and spent the rest of his career serving his country rising to the rank of General. He proudly led his troops in several campaigns and peace-keeping missions around the world with his accomplishments reported in various news media. In one news article, he was described as "America's Defender." He spent his career protecting America's national interests until his retirement a year ago.

Ray pondered on the career paths the three of them took. They were different, yet all had semblances of who they really were in high school— men *determined to make a difference in this world by helping others.* Ray thought about the thousands of patients he had guided and supported throughout his lifetime. He had been fortunate to have alleviated pain and extended lives of so many. Sergio taught thousands of students over the years and helped them achieve their ambitions. Glenn led thousands of troops through many missions and protected the lives of millions of Americans.

It was interesting to see how their lives and careers had turned out, and it made Ray think that they had really all pursued careers in service, devoting their lives to helping others.

He heard a sound in the driveway. His friends had arrived in Sergio's car. Ray picked up his bags and walked to meet them.

They gave each other big hugs. It was a long overdue in-person reunion and a very meaningful one. While they had parted ways geographically as they embarked on their respective life journeys as young men, they had remained as close as possible, communicating frequently about life—its opportunities, challenges, and outcomes both personally and professionally. Now, they have all met again in person as old men in the twilight of their lives. There would be much to talk about during this summer vacation. And yes—they have time.

Glenn opened the door for Ray,

Ray, please meet my granddaughter, Ava. As I mentioned, she will guide us to the summer home. Liza and Ava's twin brother Allan are already there. Liza wanted Ava to be with me in the car ride to their summer home to ensure that I take my medications on time and that I don't eat or drink all of the wrong things on the way there. A tall order, indeed!

All four laughed joyously!

Ray shook Ava's hand, "Pleased to meet you, Ava. Glenn's granddaughter is our granddaughter too. The three of us are like brothers. Right, Sergio?"

Sergio looked back from the driver's seat with a wide smile, "I agree 100 percent, plus we all could really use a 'chaperone'."

The men laughed.

Glenn added,

By the way, Ava just graduated from college with a degree in International Relations. She's contemplating a service career as a diplomat. Her twin brother, Allan, just completed a Business Management degree and he's interested in a corporate career in customer service. They both just started job hunting and have been asking me for career advice. But, heck what does an old general know?

Sergio quickly jumped in,

A lot! I think it was Martin Luther King, Jr. who said something like—*Knowledge is a process of piling up facts, wisdom lies in its simplification.* We've done a lot and seen a lot in our careers. We have built up a lot of knowledge. Now, we have the opportunity to simplify our learned lessons and convey it to the next generation.

Ray smiled,

Well said. You may have something there, Sergio. Also, while we've recently retired, we continue to be active in our careers as board members, consultants, and advisors. We continue to grow and give back in somewhat different ways. We are still very much involved and socially connected. We're still in the game, maybe even the top of our game. I mean look at us. Nothing here looks old! At least not that much on the outside.

The men laughed.

Ray continued, "Ava, we'd be happy to give you and Allan a few career pointers. As Glenn's grandchildren, you are part of our family, and we'd love to see you succeed."

Ava was excited,

Thank you so much! I'm all ears. I'm sure Allan will be thrilled. From what grandpa told me, you have all reached the top of your careers and service was the primary component regardless of your fields of work. There is so much Allan and I can learn from you and we're looking forward to it.

Sergio was curious, "Wait, wasn't Liza—your mom—in customer service too?"

Ava nodded, "Yes, she works as Vice President for Customer Service for a major retail chain."

Sergio turned to Ava and said, "I thought I heard Glenn mention that a few years ago. It looks like service runs in the veins of your family—grandfather, mom, and now the grandchildren too!"

Ava smiled, "I guess it does."

Glenn moved toward the back seat of the car and then said, "Ray, you have the front seat. I'll sit in the back with Ava."

"You sure?" Ray asked.

"Sure" Glenn said, "Bonding time with the granddaughter."

Ray got in the car,

Ava, by the way congratulations on your recent graduation. I'm sure you worked hard. Just like your grandfather and mother, you and Allan have both chosen admirable career paths that aim to serve others. I can't wait to hear all about your school adventures, the choice of a major and your plans for the first steps in your career!

"Thank you." Ava said, "It seemed like the natural thing to do—focus on how I could serve and support others. It wasn't a difficult decision at all."

Glenn adjusted his seat,

You know Ava, during our high school days, I don't think any of us knew that we were going to embark on careers that would or could or should have such a focus on service. We knew we liked people. We were always respectful and were ready to lend a helping hand to others. I guess service was in our DNA but we didn't plan to build a life's work on it. The career angle just fell into place naturally.

We all come from very hard-working and proud families who fought for everything they achieved from a high school education to jobs that they chose to view as careers. They instilled in us that there was nothing we couldn't achieve and that reaching our dreams was a pursuit they supported and even insisted on.

Ray closed the door,

Something about service just came to mind. I already have one career insight for you, Ava. Service is largely about helping others, and it has to come from deep within. Your grandfather, Sergio, and I have lived fulfilling lives with very different work focus. We all ended up helping others and tried our utmost to make the world a better place. Once you get to our age, you look back and realize that a life of service makes you feel good now because you spent the bulk of it bringing value to the lives of others. A career in service, regardless of what venue in which it takes place—government, private sector, or nonprofit—is actually an opportunity to offer the best version of yourself to assist others and make a meaningful and lasting impact. You can make this happen in almost any occupation. You can and should *add value to the world* as part of any job you will have.

Ava smiled at Ray and said, "Thank you, I will remember that. One question—was there one particular defining moment or event in your life when you realized you were meant for a career in service, or was it a series of events?"

Ray gave it a thought,

Good question. Hmmm…I guess it started the moment when I realized the joy I felt learning about medicine. I was fortunate to have found learning about medicine easy and enjoyable but I also developed a passion for it. It didn't seem like work at all. I felt I was meant to heal others.

Sergio tapped into the GPS and then chimed in,

It was the same for me. Once I found my calling in the field of education, everything seemed so easy. I enjoyed every minute teaching students and doing my research. But, education wasn't my first career. I first worked in sales. Sometimes, the path to a service career isn't always a straight one. But you can and must learn things from your early employment journeys so that they help make you even better. As a salesman, I first learned to sell products. Later, as a professor I used what I previously learned to inspire students and sell ideas in the classroom.

Quickly in my early employment as a salesperson, I realized that there are always opportunities to learn something new, relearn something I had heard or experienced but put in the back of my mind and unlearn strategies that were just not working (and perhaps never did)!

Sergio started the car and their summer adventure together had begun. After completing a right turn, he said,

Through my personal experience and conversations with numerous corporate executives over my career, I have learned that employees who go out of their way to *help others inside and outside the organization* stand out and have greater opportunity to continue their influence through growing levels of authority.

Glenn gave the matter some thought and added,

In the military, what you do goes around quickly. Those who consistently do a good job and are typically always available and willing to help others get a lot of respect. Years back, I had a sergeant on my staff whom everyone absolutely loved. They would have taken a bullet for the guy if they were in battle together. You know, his secret for likability and influence —*uncompromising willingness to help*. Be it day or night, rain or shine, on or off duty—if someone came to him for help, he would always do everything he could for them.

"It sounds like I learned my first lessons about service," Ava said,

Service is about wholeheartedly embracing the idea of helping others. We may not exactly know where that assistance will lead or when the right time is—but, deep in our heart and soul, we know it's the right thing to do and it would feel very satisfying, right?

Also, I am never done keeping myself current and must always be open to new information. Old information serves as a reminder that I need to let go of habits that no longer serve me or anyone else.

Ray smiled, "Absolutely! You're a fast learner! We can all learn more about service, about each other, and about life in this summer vacation. Learning is never over!"

Ava stared at the window. It crossed her mind that this trip may not be as boring as she thought it would be. Maybe she can learn a thing or two from these gentlemen. Hopefully, uncover some of the secrets behind their success.

Mastering Customer Service

Insight 1: Helping Others Constitutes the Core of Service

Introduction to Customer Satisfaction

Everyone who works in any organization has customers to serve. Some staff deal directly with customers in roles, such as sales, technical support, or customer service, but many staff have little or no contact with people we traditionally call customers. They may be in Finance, HR, R&D, or Operations, but in practice, they too have customers—internal customers. Everything they do helps another colleague or team to contribute more to the organization. Sometimes, there may be a long chain of internal customers that leads to the satisfaction of an external customer. This book is about how all those people can give better service to their internal or external customers. But first, we should explain why that is so important.

The simple answer is that **improving service to make customers more satisfied** benefits everyone. This isn't a new idea. We can trace its origins to the 18th century when Adam Smith explained that since human beings continually strive to maximize their "utility" (get the greatest benefit for the least cost), they migrate gradually, but inexorably, to the companies that come closest to delivering it[1]. In other words, they search out and stay with companies that **do best what matters most to customers,** and customer satisfaction is the phrase commonly used to encapsulate this phenomenon.

Consequently, the more gratifying the customer experience is, the more likely they are to repeat it, and vice versa. This has been demonstrated at the macro level by American Customer Satisfaction Index (ACSI) data, showing that in the United States, changes in customer satisfaction have accounted for more of the variation in future spending growth than have any other factors including income or consumer confidence[2]. In other words, if American consumers are more satisfied generally by the things the American economy is delivering to them (and by the way in which they are delivered), their rate of spending increases. If their satisfaction goes down, so does their spending and the country's economic growth.

It is now widely accepted that while the ultimate goal of a private sector company may be to deliver profits to shareholders, it will be achieved through delivering results to customers[3]. This is based on the fundamental psychological principle that people will want more of the experiences that give them pleasure while avoiding the unpleasing or dissonant experiences[4]. It explains why it is more profitable to keep existing customers than to win new ones—five times more profitable on average, according to figures released by the American Department of Consumer Affairs as long ago as 1986. Customer retention is more profitable than customer acquisition because the value of customers typically increases over time[5]. **Summarized by Harvard as the 3Rs (retention, related sales, and referrals) and based on 30 years of research, Harvard concluded that "loyal" customer behaviors explain differences in companies' financial performance more than any other factor[3]. Harvard and others have also pointed out that customer satisfaction is the main driver of customer loyalty[3,6,7].**

You would think that all this evidence, over many years about the benefits of customer satisfaction, would have resulted in all organizations now providing great service and delighting their customers. But nothing could be further from the truth. Inexplicably, customer satisfaction is not improving. A recent survey by PwC[8] based on 15,000 customer interviews across 12 countries found that **54 percent of U.S. consumers stated that customer experience at most companies needed improving**. The study found an "expectation-experience" gap across all industries—in other words, service fell short of what customers expected. The biggest gap was in air travel where experience was 33 percent below expectation. Examples of other sector gaps include retail 21 percent, banking 20 percent, insurance 18 percent, and restaurants 12 percent. This is serious because in most developed economies, customers now have a vast array of choices for most products and services, and with expectations rising, they are becoming more intolerant of poor service. **In the United States, 59 percent will walk away after several bad experiences and 17 percent after just one bad experience. In Latin America, a huge 47 percent will**

switch after one bad experience and 30 percent on average across all the countries surveyed.

But as well as threats to organizations that deliver poor service, there are opportunities for those who deliver great service. The benefits of customer loyalty first summarized by Harvard as long ago as in the 1990s[9] have been confirmed by the PwC survey. They found that **if you deliver great service that makes customers highly satisfied, you will have loyal customers who will keep coming back, will buy other products and services from you, and they will recommend you to others.** But there is another, less well-known opportunity highlighted by the PwC report—earning a price premium. Customers will pay a higher price if companies give them a great experience, and the report quantifies this price premium across various sectors. So, for example, giving great service can win a 16 percent price premium for coffee restaurants, 14 percent for hotels, 12 percent for restaurants, 10 percent for airlines, and 7 percent for insurance companies.

This book will provide insights into how to deliver great service and how to monitor customers' views to ensure that it results in higher customer satisfaction.

CHAPTER 2

Take Time to Understand

The best way to find yourself is to lose yourself in the service of others.
—Mahatma Gandhi, Indian Lawyer

The driving time from Ray's hometown in Illinois to Liza's summer home in South Carolina would take about 14 hours. They had to factor in stops for restroom use and meals. The plan was to drive for eight hours then stay in a hotel somewhere before doing the final stretch to Liza's summer home.

The men figured that a road trip might be more fun than spending time in the airport. Also, they wanted to bring plenty of fishing gear since they were planning to stay in Liza's summer home for a good part of the summer.

After a few hours on the road, the quartet started to feel hungry. They decided to stop for lunch at a small-town diner.

The moment they stepped in a friendly receptionist welcomed them. She smiled warmly and said,

Hi, my name is Katie. Welcome, and thank you for visiting us today. I hope your travels are going okay. We are somewhat packed, but I'll try my hardest to get you the seats that suit you best. Do you prefer to be seated indoors or outdoors? We have a patio overlooking a pond at the back. Inside we have televisions, darts, and a pool table if you'd like to have some fun while dining.

Ray looked at the group, "Well, what are your preferences?" It was a quick unanimous decision. "We'll have outdoor seating please."

Katie extended her arm to the right, "Sure, follow me please. Are these seats OK for you all?"

Katie helped everyone with their seats and made sure they were comfortable saying, "Enjoy your time here. A waiter will be with you shortly. Before I go, would you like me to raise the umbrella over your table since it's a pretty sunny day?"

About two minutes later, Katie returned with a large canvas bag.

I brought you some bug spray, sunscreen lotion and hand sanitizer. Please let me know if you need anything else. Also, the blue and red buzzers by the table are to call for assistance. Red for me and blue for your waiter. Your waiter is Bob, and he will be here shortly with glasses of water and a welcome basket of fruits and snacks. He will also take your order whenever you're ready. I hope you have a fantastic meal and thanks for dining with us!

Sergio was wide-eyed, "I think I just experienced the best restaurant welcome in my life. And, that's saying a lot because I've been to many restaurants around the world."

Ray agreed, "Heck, if that's the way they treat customers as they enter, I wonder what the food tastes like."

Glenn laughed,

The receptionist, Katie was it? Well, she certainly made us all feel special. Her big radiant smile conveyed so much joy and sincerity. There's something very genuine with the way she talked and carried herself. It was authentic hospitality. She made us all feel like VIPs. Ray, did you tell them we were coming?

It was Ray's turn to laugh,

Absolutely not. Couldn't have predicted when and where we would get hungry. Never heard of this place before and we're in the middle of nowhere! I guess they treat everyone this way. The place is packed, and everybody is smiling and happy.

Ava joined in,

It was the kind of welcome that made you feel right at home and important. Katie was candid, warm, and really showed that she cared. I definitely received excellent service today from Katie and wow, when I compare it to how we are treated in the dorm cafeteria, it's all the difference in the world! I wish all food service places were like this.

As Katie mentioned, the waiter promptly showed up and introduced himself as Bob. He brought along glasses of cold water for everyone, along with small trays of fruits, nuts, and candies.

"We don't want to spoil your appetite, but in case you're hungry we'd like to offer these complimentary goodies," Bob said smiling.

Oh, and here's the menu and the beverage list. I'll give you some time to look them over. If you'd like something outside of the menu, let me know. I can't promise our chef can make your special request, but we may be able to get you something pretty close. Relax, enjoy yourselves, and just wave at me or press the blue button when you're ready to order your drinks or your meal. See you in a bit!

The group ordered their meals and were extremely delighted as they started sampling the fare.

"Well" Ray said, "It's exactly what I wanted and more. Done just like I requested. It's delicious."

Sergio concurred, "I totally agree. You know why? Bob repeated our orders and verified that he had it all down correctly. He made an effort to really know our specific preferences to make sure he met our exact needs."

Ava nodded,

Also, he took the time to meticulously capture everything in his notes. He didn't rush. He was very patient. I dislike when I go to a restaurant and they rush me to order. It makes me feel like all that mattered was the immediate sale. I was not important. I am just one of many customers.

Glenn wiped his forehead with a handkerchief and said,

I felt that way too in some restaurants. Very little patience and respect are shown. In places like that, the customers are commodities. They are not special. To the contrary, Bob asked me a lot of questions and took time to listen. He made me feel very special and important. It almost made me feel that the meal was made just for me, and it's not just a regular dish on the menu. And to top all that, they delivered a meal that exceeded expectations. As a result, that made the dining experience extraordinary and the customer service quality amazing.

Ava picked up some spilled food near Glenn's plate and put it away, "Why can't all restaurants train their people to be patient, respectful, caring, and really listen to their customers more?"

Ray folded the napkin on the table,

For many, business got in the way. Profit, work efficiency, and speed of transaction became more important than how the customer actually felt. What they forgot is that customers have choices. There are many similar businesses out there. Customers may choose not to return. As a result, their long-term business sustainability may become questionable. The owner of this restaurant is smart. Emphasis and priority was placed on customer satisfaction. Look how full the place is and how happy the customers appear. This place will thrive for a long time because of their customer-focused approach. And, by the way, in this place they don't just please the customer, they delight the customer. They deliver beyond what is expected and really impress the customer.

Sergio reinforced Ray's thoughts,

Customers here are clearly not viewed as an interruption. The owner and staff acknowledge with every interaction that having great products and average or below average service doesn't create customer loyalty. They give their best effort to everyone including fellow staff.

Ava moved her glass to the side,

The location of this restaurant is a little out of the way. Yet customers come. It looks like people are willing to travel to get here and experience their top-quality food and exceptional service. I am reminded of Apple, many of their customers are so loyal and committed. When a new product comes out, people often wait in long lines to purchase it. It looks like they really know their customers and know how to please them. As a result, the customers have become very loyal and enthusiastic patrons.

Sergio took a sip of water then said,

True. There's an important lesson about service here—*know your audience*. Once you know them well enough, you can create a product or deliver a service designed exactly toward their wishes. Also, loyalty should not be taken for granted. Customers are only loyal as long as they continue to receive consistent excellent service and products. When someone else serves them better than you, you can lose what you thought was your best customer!

Ray nodded,

So true, Sergio. I know that patients will leave me if anything in my clinic doesn't meet their expectations despite how long we've been together. To assure I know my patients well, I made an effort to study my patient's records and ask them very precise questions. That way I knew their condition better, made more accurate diagnoses and determined with them the most appropriate treatment. My patient retention record was excellent and that is because I concentrated on them—their loyalty to me and our clinic was a wonderful by-product!

"Well, it must have worked, Ray." Glenn said,

It made you one of the top doctors in America. As a General, I took the same approach. When leading my troops, I made it a point to know their strengths as well as their weaknesses. That way, when we went into battle, I knew to whom I should delegate particular tasks. This strategy helped us win battles, save lives, and successfully complete our missions. Their loyalty to me and our effort was critical and too often a matter of life and death. I had to know I had their loyalty and did everything in my power to assure they knew that I appreciated it.

Sergio added,

As a Professor, I did the same for my students. Each one of us has different learning styles—some learn better by seeing, others by hearing, and others by actually doing. So in my courses, I tried to know as much as I could about the student as well as the composition of my class. That way, as the semester progressed, I refined the activities to optimize student learning, creating an environment in which all of us thrived.

Ava joined in. "That explains the many teaching awards and recognition you received from around the world. Grandpa mentioned some of them to me when he saw them in the news or on social media. It seems like *successful service requires knowing who you serve very well and never taking their loyalty for granted.*"

"Definitely" the three men said in unison. "In fact," said Ray,

It's as important as the concept of helping others. If you don't have as complete a knowledge as possible of what's important to your customers, your best efforts to help them could misfire. You might work incredibly hard to do very well at things that don't really matter to your customer group. The *key is doing your best in what matters most.*

Sergio agreed and added another thought.

We've just witnessed that in action here today. In a small business, you can talk directly to your customers, understand their exact needs, and make sure you deliver what matters most. But in a bigger organization, where it's not feasible to talk directly to all your customers, you have to use other methods. In the hotel chain where I serve as a Board Member, we gather feedback on what's important to customers from frontline staff who do talk to customers directly and by talking to representative samples of customers. You can do that by using techniques such as focus groups for an in-depth understanding of customers' needs and customer surveys to prioritize those needs across much bigger samples. That way we can get a really good understanding of our customers' needs and priorities and use that insight to develop products and services that meet their needs.

Glenn added,

Yes, Sergio. Businesses must explore the best ways to get feedback from their customers—the most loyal and those that have left you. Comment cards work well in some businesses, seeking employee feedback on what is working and what isn't, tracking specific and meaningful service metrics reflects how you are doing over time, and even the somewhat questionable use of "secret shoppers" can tell you what you need to know. The key is don't seek feedback you don't intend to use!

Mastering Customer Service

Insight 2: Take the Time to Understand Your Customers

Understanding Customers

Understanding your customers' needs and priorities is the essential starting point for delivering good service. Katie understood this at the Diner when, after a warm welcome, she proceeded to ask the group questions to understand their preferences before seating them. When Ava expressed her wish that all restaurants could be more like the Diner and listen to their customers more, Sergio agreed, saying that from his experience, companies must know their audience in order to create and deliver a product or service that exactly matches their customers' needs. Ray made the additional point that if you don't understand your customers *"your best efforts to help them could misfire. You might work incredibly hard to do very well at things that don't really matter to your customers."*

Finally, Sergio highlighted an important difference between small and large organizations. **Small businesses interact directly with their customers, so if they take the time and trouble to ask enough questions, they can develop a very good understanding of customers' priorities. In big organizations and, increasingly, in remote businesses such as online retailers, the majority of staff have no direct contact with customers, so they have to use other methods to develop enough understanding of customers.** Sergio mentioned that his hotel group used focus groups and surveys for this purpose, and, for the remainder of this section, we will outline the options for how large organizations and other companies with little or no customer contact can build a close understanding of customers' needs and priorities.

Why Do We Need to Understand Customers? It's a valid question. One could argue that rather than investing time and resources into understanding customers, why not just put all that effort into ensuring that staff deliver great service? In reality we have known the answer for many decades. Back in the 1960s, American marketing guru Philip Kotler was telling us how to make customers satisfied. *"If the product matches expectations, the consumer is satisfied; if it exceeds them, the consumer is highly satisfied; if it falls short, the consumer is dissatisfied.*"[1] The crucial takeaway from this definition is that the customer's satisfaction judgment is a relative concept. In other words, it's not just based on an objective assessment of the supplier's performance, but it's also strongly influenced by what the customer had expected in the first place. The supplier's performance might be good by any objective standard, but if the customer had expected something even better, they will not be completely satisfied and may go elsewhere next time they need that product or service.

The University of Michigan Business School has developed our understanding of how customer satisfaction works in more recent years, especially with the introduction of one crucial concept—*the lens of the customer* versus *the lens of the organization.*[2] They point out that suppliers and their customers often do not see things in the same way. Suppliers typically think in terms of the products or services they supply, the people they employ to provide them, and the processes they use to deliver the product or service. Customers look at things from their own perspective, focusing on what they want out of that transaction or experience, basing their evaluation of suppliers on whether they have received the results, outcomes, or benefits they expected. **So if customers' satisfaction judgments are based on the extent to which their requirements have been met, the only way suppliers can ever satisfy their customers enough to retain their loyalty is to have a complete understanding of what those requirements are.** So how do you develop that understanding?

Qualitative Research.   This is large organizations' equivalent of talking to customers and asking them questions. Most large organizations use a specialist agency as they will have relevant expertise, and it is more efficient than employing permanent staff for the purpose. Qualitative research involves getting a lot of information from a small number of customers, typically around 30 to 60. This can be done using focus groups or depth interviews, either of which can be conducted face to face or online. A depth interview is with an individual customer and will last up to one hour. A focus group typically involves eight customers and takes at least 90 minutes. Neither approach is better or worse, but focus groups tend to be a more efficient use of time and benefit from the interaction between the customers, stimulating more thoughts and experiences. In both cases, the moderator's role is to get customers talking in detail about their experiences, attitudes, emotions, and feelings when they use the product or service in question. From these discussions, the moderator can draw out everything that is of any importance to customers. Usually there are very many things, but of course, they're not all equally important. Some are more important than others. So the next step is to prioritize. What are the "must-haves" and what are just "nice-to-haves?" This process can be started with depth interview and focus group participants, but to arrive at a reliable understanding of the relative importance of customers' requirements, you need to involve a lot more customers. This is quantitative research, which we will describe very briefly next.

Quantitative Research.   To reach a reliable understanding of the relative importance of customers' requirements, it is necessary to involve many more customers, usually at least 200 and, for some organizations, 1,000 or more customers who have had recent experience with the organization. This has to be done through large-scale quantitative surveys which can be self-completion, typically online, or interviews, usually conducted by telephone. Questionnaires do have to be quite long since all the customer requirements that have been identified in the exploratory research must be prioritized. To do this, the customers must be asked to rate all the requirements for importance. Opinions on how to do this do vary, but we recommend asking customers to score them for importance on a 10-point numerical scale. This is a very straight forward process simply done by asking participants to give each requirement a score out of 10 for how important it is to them personally. The outcome is known as "stated importance." Then all the requirements have to be scored on the same scale for satisfaction. This enables the researcher to calculate a measure of "derived importance," which is done by using correlation or regression techniques. Stated importance is a measure of how important customers say things are and tends to overemphasize givens. Thinking of the Diner, givens such as "cleanliness of the restaurant" or "speed of service" will always be given very high importance scores by customers. Derived importance measures can uncover hidden differentiators which subconsciously might have a strong influence on customers' decision about where to go next time they eat out. Examples for the diner might be "recognition of returning customers" or "nutritional information about dishes."

By putting the two measures together, organizations will get a truly rounded measure of what's important to customers. This is best achieved on a total importance matrix with stated importance on the y-axis and derived importance on the x-axis. The requirements closest to the top right-hand corner of the matrix are the ones that are most important to customers. For a much more thorough explanation of how to identify what matters most to customers including full details about stated and derived importance and the total importance matrix see Hill, Roche and Allen: "Customer Satisfaction: The Customer Experience Through the Customer's Eyes."[3]

Doing Best What Matters Most.   As we established in Chapter 1, being helpful and employing staff who want to help others is the essential starting point for delivering great service. But it's not enough. **Even the best staff working incredibly hard to be as helpful as they can might not make customers very satisfied if they don't really understand what matters most to customers. Delivering great service isn't just about doing your best, it's about doing best what matters most to customers. And to do that companies need an excellent understanding of what does matter most to customers.**

CHAPTER 3

"Live" the Mission

Every person above the ordinary has a certain mission that they are called to fulfill.
—Johann Wolfgang von Goethe, German Author

After the wonderful experience at the restaurant, the group continued on their trip.

With Sergio in the driver's seat, the three men reminisced and laughed at their high school experiences. They talked about their poverty and how they assembled a car together in order to get around. They even drove to a nearby city to find a thrift shop for their prom attire. Those were hungry days that posed many challenges but transformed them into strong men.

As the group laughed at the experiences of their youth, they heard a loud bang. The front right tire had exploded. The truck slid and fell into a shallow creek.

Sergio was concerned, "Is everyone okay?"

Everyone responded positively.

Sergio stepped out of the truck and said, "So sorry about that."

"Hey" Glenn responded, "No need to apologize. It's not your fault. These things happen. You did a great job in keeping the truck upright. I'm not sure I could have done that maneuver."

Sergio surveyed the damage, "We may need a tow truck."

Ray was a bit pessimistic, "Might be a challenge. It's late Saturday afternoon and a holiday weekend. Nearby auto shops might be closed at this time. All we can do is try."

They were in a remote area, and the nearest auto shop was about 10 miles away according to the internet.

Ray called using his mobile phone and put it on speaker, so everyone could follow the conversation.

The phone rang about 10 times, and no one picked up. Ray tried again, and on the fifth ring, someone answered.

"Ronnie's Auto Shop, good evening. This is Ron." The voice was that of someone who sounded tired and was panting like he had been interrupted from some heavy manual work, but he managed to convey a calm and friendly demeanor.

"Ron" Ray said, "This is Ray Richardson. Sorry to call you so late on a Saturday. We had a car mishap and need a tow truck and some mechanical help. Might you be able to assist? We're about 10 miles away."

Ron hesitated, "We're actually closed, and my three guys are gone for the day. Wait, I see one of the guys—Phil—just pulling up in the driveway. I'll ask him. Hold for a bit."

The quartet waited tensely. Camping in the car in this remote place for the night was not appealing.

Ron got back on the phone, "You're in luck. Phil has a previous commitment, but he'll cancel it to help you out. We're a small shop, but we have a motto that we live by, *'We help by all means.'* I hope we live up to it every day, but for sure, today, we definitely will."

The group was ecstatic. They explained the problem and gave general directions to their location.

Since the repairs would probably run late into the night, Ron recommended that they stay in the town's only bed and breakfast—Holly's. He offered to make the arrangements, and Phil said he would drop them off there before he headed to the shop to do the repairs. Ron offered to bring the truck to Holly's once the work was done the next day.

The group gratefully accepted.

In about 30 minutes, Phil arrived with the tow truck.

"Phil, thank you so much for doing this" Ray said.

Phil smiled graciously, "Happy to do so. We are a small firm, but we take our mission seriously. We do all we can to help our customers."

Sergio was impressed, "Phil, your *concept of service* is far more impressive and meaningful than many of the multinational corporations

I have dealt with. It's *clear, simple, real, and most importantly, lived.* You really helped us out today, Phil. Thank you so much."

Phil shrugged off the compliment,

We do this all the time. You're most welcome. We believe in a *strong culture of excellent service and know we have to live it every day even when it's not convenient.* That's what makes us stand out in this region as one of the top car repair businesses. We're very proud of that.

As Phil started to put the towing system in place, Ava turned to the three men, "Looks like there's another service lesson here. *Support your organization's mission and culture faithfully. Not just when it's convenient or noticeable to the public. Integrity is doing the right thing even when no one is watching."*

Ray agreed,

You're exactly right. Some organizations have *developed and nurtured the right culture for exceptional customer service—it defines them. It shapes everything they think, say, and do* and becomes a basis for action. Eventually, it becomes a guide on the way they do things—from the smallest seemingly unimportant decisions to the biggest plans.

Ava started to arrange some of the displaced items in the truck, "The values and culture that these customer-oriented companies have—do you think they had them from the start-up of the organization or did they develop it over time?"

Sergio assisted her in arranging the items,

Great question. Based on my experience and the research I've read, the *values, and day-to-day behaviors of the founder and the leadership team of the company have a way of shaping the ultimate organizational culture.* The founder and the leaders from the early stage of the business have ideally communicated their beliefs and positively reinforced certain behaviors. This then evolved into a mindset, a way of behaving, and hopefully ended up in their motto, slogan, and even policy and training manuals. Founders and leaders who have an inherent passion to please customers consciously and subconsciously passed this on to the entire organization.

Ray gave the matter some thought,

I agree, Sergio. *Having the attitude of service, the knowledge to do the job needed, and the empowerment to go above and beyond are the keys to excellent customer service.* You know, Chick-fil-A is an example of a company that prioritizes their customers. I've heard of cases where the staff went out of their way to help customers carry heavy trays or gave free nuggets for a customer's pet.

Ava was impressed,

Wow. Given Chick-fil-A is a large organization, it must have taken a huge effort and investment on the part of the company to get everyone on board attitudinally and to train and empower them to consistently deliver exceptional customer service.

Sergio smiled,

That's another reason why founders and leaders have to believe exceptional customer service matters. The leadership team gets to allocate their resources on initiatives that they believe are important to their customers and business. If customer service is close to their hearts to begin with, investment in building customer satisfaction would be a no-brainer for them.

Ava turned to Sergio,

Do you think company cultures and values could or should change over time—to keep up with the current world or to correct elements of the culture that just aren't working? If a company started with little emphasis on customer service, can they do a turnaround?

Sergio quickly responded,

Definitely, smart companies do exactly that. Upon realization that customers aren't coming back unless the organization makes a change because competitors are doing a better job at customer service, companies must make a dramatic change. They begin a cultural change or transformation process. It's not always easy, and it takes serious time and commitment. But, it can be done.

Ray jumped in,

I would add that *companies need to be constantly changing to please their customers.* Customers' values and expectations evolve over time, and companies need to be able to adapt and make adjustments to respond to these changes. *Customers are constantly comparing your business to any other positive experience they had at other companies whether they are in the same field as your business or not.* Loyalty is fleeting, and the values and the culture a company possesses set a solid foundation for actions and decisions that will retain your customers and attract new ones. *Constantly updating the purposefulness of your culture, values, and associated behaviors is critical to the business's ongoing success.*

Ray looked at Glenn to see if he was alright. He seemed quiet. Glenn picked up what Ray was thinking and yawned,

No, I haven't dozed off yet. Your discussion on values, culture, and mission brought back some memories from my military career. We embraced a culture of service in the military, and, often times, we pursued our mission at all costs. At times, supporting the needs of the government meant sacrificing personal ambitions and desires. There were times I took on assignments I didn't like in order to serve the greater good. We're all one large team, and it's been about making changes to serve the needs of others at any given moment. The culture in the military is truly "one for all and all for one." I'm proud of that and enjoyed living it every day.

"I did the same in academia." Sergio said.

As a professor, aside from teaching, we had to publish in journals to support and advance scholarship. Sure, it brings some recognition for oneself, but it also leads to organizational prestige and is essential for accreditation purposes. The publishing work academics do helps build a body of knowledge for all to learn from and grow. In addition, professors serve on several internal and external committees to achieve institutional goals.

Ray concurred,

Me as well. As a doctor, I provided support on two levels—for my patients and my private health and wellness company. Both efforts are demanding and require significant sacrifices. But if you believe in your organization, your role in it, the people counting on you, and the importance of your contribution, it becomes an easy task. Employees in all professions at all levels make remarkable organizational contributions every day in both the public and private sectors. A *mindset anchored in support for others* elevates the quality and level of service. Today, Ronnie's Auto Shop provided a perfect example of a well-defined and consistently implemented *culture of service.*

Mastering Customer Service

Insight 3: "Live" Your Organization's Mission With Every Interaction

"Living" Your Organization's Mission

The most critical step in being able to live your organization's mission is having **arrived at your own mission and related vision and values first,** which allows you to appropriately assess every organization you are considering joining to see if there is enough of a match that you feel comfortable in choosing them as your employer.

Once you have accepted and are in any role with any company, you are now serving others, so you are a **"customer service professional."** We see the epitome of that concept with Ron and Phil and their Auto Shop philosophy: "*We help by all means.*" **Clear, simple, real, and, most importantly, lived** are the keys to a likely successful mission statement. While it was late and the shop was "closed" with employees gone for the day, Ron and Phil put their mantra into action by jumping at the opportunity to not only retrieve the travelers' car and repair it but also "retrieve" the travelers themselves taking them to a nearby Bed and Breakfast for the night to assure their comfort while awaiting the car repairs.

Ava discussed the **service lesson** all four of them were reminded of that day: Regardless of one's job description, we all have, as our primary function, **to support our organization's mission and culture faithfully. Not just when it's convenient or noticeable to the public. Living with integrity at every interaction—doing the right thing even when no one is watching.** Ray goes on to emphasize that **developing and nurturing the right culture for exceptional customer service defines your organization**—it shapes everything your organization thinks, says, and does and becomes the basis for every action.

Three Points Within This Chapter Deserve Special Consideration

Why Is Your Organization's Mission Important?

According to the U.S. Bureau of Labor Statistics, **less than 50 percent of start-up companies survive through their fifth year,** and research done by McKinsey & Company and the University of Minnesota found that **companies with a clear and concise mission statement are more likely to outperform their competitors.** Similarly, *Harvard Business Review* reports that **companies with a clearly defined and communicated mission statement have higher levels of employee engagement and loyalty.** Additionally, **63 percent of employees at companies with solid mission statements report being motivated versus 31 percent at other companies.** So, it is clear that developing, implementing, and assuring compliance with your company's mission statement is critical to your personal success and that of the company you support.

A mission statement answers the question **"what do we do?"** by:[1]

- **Being concise, clear, realistic, easy to understand,** and that is well aligned with the organization's overall strategy and objectives.
- **Clarifying the business's purpose and goals by communicating** its core values; the target audience and outlining primary products, services, and activities.
- **Fostering understanding and support by the employee group** at large about how their work contributes to the organization's success.
- **Helping customers, investors, and other stakeholders understand** what the company does.
- **Describing why the company exists.**
- **Emphasizing how the business is different** from competitors.

Your business's mission statement, as developed per the criteria above, will drive the overall vision of your company as well as the subsequent values that fill your "hallways" every day with respectful, productive, and focused interactions.

Why Do We Need an Attitude of Service?

Excellent customer service starts with you—how you truly feel about providing the best service you can with every interaction. Having the **attitude of service, the knowledge to do the job needed, and the empowerment to go above and beyond are the keys to excellent customer service.**

The debate is alive and well regarding whether empowerment, as it relates to customer service decisions, should be greater at the direct service level. Many organizations have a **tiered structure, which forces customers to work their way up the chain** to get what they feel they need/deserve as it relates to the product/service in question. That leaves front-line staff with the inability to solve the customer's issue many times. Instead, they have to elevate it to a Supervisor, Manager, Director, and so on.[2]

To say that it is frustrating to the customer is probably an understatement. **Most customers just want their issue addressed as simply and quickly as possible without having to tell their story over and over to those higher up in the chain of command.** Plus, there is often a wait time for someone to whom the issue was referred to get back to the customer. And, of course, there are those times where the issue isn't a priority to the person to whom it was referred, and so the customer remains the point person to assure that the issue is followed up on in a timely fashion. **It feels as if the ball is always in the customer's court with the tiered approach to resolving customer issues and that is not the best component to assure loyalty to your business.**

The question on the table is whether a tiered level of empowerment truly reflects an attitude of service. Even if corporate design is out of our control, **every employee regardless of their job description must embrace the truly empowering concept that part of our job is to do our best to provide optimal customer service with every interaction. That can only happen if the employee has the attitude of excellent service.**

Feeling proud of who you are, the role you play, and the importance of your interaction with every customer starts with feeling good about yourself. You owe it to you, your organization

and co-workers, and certainly your customers to bring your best self to work every day.

Do Customers Remain Yours Forever?

Loyalty is fleeting. In reality, customers are NOT yours for a lifetime. There is some likelihood that they may only be loyal to you/your organization through the next interaction with you! Despite the positive relationship you may have developed with a customer—perhaps for years—it can be gone in an instant because they are **not only comparing your service to a competitor in the same line of business as you but also to any service/product they have just received from any business!**

In actuality, you are competing with every company with whom your customer does business. If your customer just received optimal service from their Oil Change company and then come, next, to you for service, they are comparing you to the positive experience at the Oil Change company because that is uppermost in their mind. **It takes a "lifetime" to create a relationship of trust with a customer, and it can be lost in a minute!**

And, too often, you/the organization may not know why. Many customers just leave a company with whom they have been doing business—sometimes for years—without sharing why with you. They will, however, quite likely share their (often exaggerated) reasons for leaving with others, and in this day of social media, it can hit thousands of people quickly.

Some interesting statistics regarding customer feelings about service quality: **83 percent** of consumers agree that **good customer service will turn them from one-time shoppers into lifers; 90 percent** of customers base **brand loyalty on the quality of customer service; 76 percent** of customers **will leave a business for good after the second negative experience; 72 percent** of customers are ready to **share a good experience** with others, and **62 percent will share a bad experience** with others; **90 percent** of customers **want an immediate response** when they have a customer service question, and for **33 percent, waiting on hold is the most frustrating part** of customer service; **80** percent of customers say **experience is equally as important as the company's products or services.**[3]

Constantly updating the purposefulness of your organization's culture, values, and associated behaviors is critical to the business's ongoing success. Your personal duty is to maintain the kind of relationship with your customers that will **weather an occasional breakdown**—because they will happen from time to time—but remain secure and loyal with your **consistent positive attitude of service, playing out your values of respect every day with every interaction. Customers expect and deserve your competency AND your positive attitude.**[4] **Customers are always presenting you with an opportunity to serve. If you don't take advantage of that opportunity, someone else will!**[5]

CHAPTER 4

Identify and Deliver a Consistent High-Value Proposition

Strive not to be a success but rather to be of value.

—Albert Einstein, Theoretical Physicist

While Phil had been recovering the vehicle and the four travelers, Ron had organized overnight accommodations for the group with a local lady that he knew who had a Bed and Breakfast. Phil kindly dropped them off there.

Holly Avery welcomed the group from the porch of her farmhouse. Ron told them that it was a spacious eight-bedroom house that was passed on to Holly through her family starting with her great-grand-father. She had lived all of her life in that house as had her father, grandfather, and great-grandfather. With her husband, Tom, long gone, and her three children having found careers out of town, she was the sole keeper of the property. To a large extent, the house retained the character of a prosperous early 1900's home.

Ron also mentioned that Holly has continued to manage the operations of a large farm along with the house. From time to time, she opens her home to stranded travelers and local tourists. She keeps the house impeccably clean at all times and is always ready for surprise guests. Visitors have been a welcome break from her rather solitary life. She always makes it a practice to shower every single guest with the warmth and affection of a doting mother.

"Welcome, everyone," she said enthusiastically, "I'm so happy to see you. Ron told me about your car troubles. Hopefully, your vehicle will be up and running soon. Meanwhile, please make yourselves at home."

In the dining room, Holly had cookies and lemonade ready and made it a point to get to know each of them, telling the quartet about her home's history.

Once everyone had relaxed a bit, Holly took them to their respective rooms.

"Well, please get settled, and in about an hour or so, I'll have a country style dinner waiting for you at the kitchen table. There will be a variety of beverages available too!"

The group expressed their appreciation, grateful they didn't have to spend the night in the woods in the car and that this wonderful local accommodation was available.

After about an hour, they gathered in the kitchen. As Holly promised, beverages and a wide array of home-cooked meal options were ready.

"Do you have guests around here often?" Ray asked.

Holly smiled,

Not as often as I want. Every visitor is extra special. Arrivals vary according to the season with the majority being from out of town, visiting family members nearby. And, there are a few cases like yours, which I thoroughly enjoy.

Ray sipped on his beer and said,

We're so lucky to have found you, and I'm sure your other guests are equally pleased to find a clean, comfortable, and friendly place to stay. How you've preserved the place is amazing! It feels like I've stumbled back in time.

Sergio had started sampling some of the dishes,

By the way, the food is awesome. There's nothing like a warm, home-cooked meal at the end of a rough day. Your place really offers a very *high-value proposition*, and I'll never forget it. You've got the highest level of hospitality, a welcoming and warm smile, amazing ambience, great food and drinks, and cozy bedrooms. What else would a weary traveler ask for? This place is like heaven on earth for any traveler. Thank you so much for accommodating us at such a short notice.

Holly opened the oven and took out a freshly baked apple pie, "Oh, the pleasure is mine. It can get lonely around here, and I enjoy the occasional company. I've learned so much from my guests and made many friends over the years."

Ava was curious, "Has your place been written about in travel magazines or perhaps mentioned in social media? What do you do for sales and marketing?"

Holly laughed self-consciously,

No, no, dear. I don't do any of those things. I don't spend a single cent on sales and marketing. All of our PR is solely by word of mouth. When my guests are happy, they tell their friends and family, and soon after, we get visitors from all over the country. There were a few times we even had visitors from overseas. Someone mentioned our place to foreign travelers in the plane or on a train ride. And they came to visit us! They wanted to experience American small-town hospitality, and they must have liked it. They ended up staying for a few weeks!

Ava smiled, "You do have quite a beautiful place. A hidden gem." Holly started to brew some hot tea,

Maybe we're a little too hidden. But I guess that's what makes our place somewhat special. It's not for everyone. But, it's very meaningful and delightful for some. I've discovered that people make choices about where they will stay as a repeat customer— they *don't have to do business with me, and so my best PR is doing everything within my power to assure they have the most memorable stay possible that specifically meets their needs and wants.* That keeps me on my toes, and I enjoy that challenge.

Ava walked over to assist her,

That might just be the secret to your success. It's not just about serving everyone—which is hard to do anyway—but *serving the audience at that moment in an exceptional way so that they are not just pleased but delighted.*

Holly started to pour the tea into cups, "Hot tea anyone? You are such a smart young woman, Ava. I'm sure you'll have an amazing career."

Sergio and Ray thanked Holly and helped themselves to the hot tea. Holly continued,

There is one other thing that I think has been instrumental to my business success. That is—taking pride in what I do. While I have a beautiful place, it wouldn't be half as exciting for others to visit unless I have a passion for entertaining people, for cooking, for cleaning, for decorating, and doing the other small but important things that make their stay memorable. There's a lot of work in running a place like this, but everything is easy for me because I love what I do and take pride in every single chore. I think this sense of pride has helped me do a better job running the place and caring for my customers.

Sergio took a sip of his tea,

I heard a quote once that said something like this—"customer service is not a department, it's an attitude." Building on the *positive attitude pertaining to pride of work and the desire to delight others can make all the difference.*

Ray moved toward the table, "Amen to that. Shall we enjoy this amazing meal?"

The quartet laughed and started dinner. They praised Holly for the wonderful cuisine. As they proceeded with their meal, they swapped stories about their experiences living a rural life in their youth.

After dinner, the group moved to the front porch with their beverages. They gazed at the starlit sky and breathed in the cool country air.

Glenn sat in one of the rocking chairs, "I've forgotten how wonderful country living can be. It's lovely out here."

Ava gazed at the well-lit sky, "It seems so bright around here. The stars are literally glowing."

Sergio stood beside her and said, "This place is special, and so is Holly."

Ray had a thought, "You mentioned value proposition earlier. This place offers the entire package—excellent venue, gracious hostess, great food, and availability in time of need. This place delivers an exceptional service through the overall value it offers."

Sergio agreed,

Offering value definitely ties in closely to the notion of service. *The most successful companies out there make sure they offer an ongoing and constantly improving unique value to their customers.* As a Professor, I am constantly doing research or publishing to assure I always add value to my students and those reading my works.

"Yes" agreed Ray, "An example is my wellness business which offers free health and lifestyle checks to all customers who become members. From then on, as they wish, we give them regular health and lifestyle advice."

Glenn stood up to stretch,

Come to think of it. The same principle applies to service careers. To move up the organization's ladder, you need to offer consistently high value, and it must continue to grow over time as you gain more experience and develop new skills. In my years in the military, I honed my skills and constantly sought ways to add value. I guess it was second nature to me so I was fortunate, but everyone can learn and apply that skill. We can't forget that you *have to have the attitude of service at your fingertips at every interaction.*

Ray pondered the conversation adding, "In the medical field, it's the same. As doctors, we need to continually upgrade our knowledge to assure we offer the best value and service to our patients as individuals."

Ava stood up and took a closer look at the beautiful evening sky,

My mom has had a long career in customer service in the corporate world, and she used to say, 'The purpose of business should be to make life better for people.' I now understand that a big part of making life better for people is finding the optimal ways to really provide impactful and lasting value.

Ava processed the conversation they just had. She soon realized that, as the stars in the sky provide value in terms of beauty and light, service businesses and the people in those careers must *strive to deliver the best value possible every day with every interaction because customers are never yours for any length of time. You compete to keep them with every interaction.*

Mastering Customer Service

Insight 4: Identify and Deliver a Consistent High-Value Proposition to Your Customers

Identifying and Delivering Consistent High-Value Propositions

Delivering a consistent and high-value proposition is your goal every day with every interaction. Holly said it best: "I love what I do and take pride in every single chore. I think this sense of pride has helped me do a better job running the place and caring for my customers." Holly is a role model for anticipating what a high-value proposition should look like and delivering it to her customers with joy and pride.

And Sergio drives home the point by saying: "**Customer service is not a department, it's an attitude.**" If your organization has a "customer service department," that may be your first problem. Customer service is everyone's primary duty. Getting the **Myths of Customer Service** straight in your head allows you to perform optimally with every customer.[1]

> **Myth #1: Customers are an interruption.** They are your job and never an interruption. You would not have a job were it not for customers.
>
> **Myth #2: Customers have to do business with you.** Not even internal customers have to do business with your department/function. Everything can be outsourced, and your service level should assure that the option never arises.
>
> **Myth #3: Products and services alone create customer loyalty.** OPTIMAL products and personalized services with every interaction create customer loyalty.
>
> **Myth #4: Customers will remain loyal over time.** Customers remain loyal from one interaction to the next.
>
> **Myth #5: Your service is compared only to others in similar industries.** In fact, your service is compared to the most recent experience your customer has had with any provider. Your competition is everyone out there doing business.

Myth #6: To your customers, you represent only a fraction of the company. Indeed, to your customer, when they are working with you specifically—YOU ARE THE COMPANY.

Myth #7: The customer is always right. That is highly unlikely, and your job is to listen so that you thoroughly understand their request; provide that which you can; to your level of empowerment; assess how you can better meet their request; and finally, coach the customer respectfully into another view of what you can and will provide to meet their needs/wants.

Holly lives the positive sides of these myths with her every interaction with the mantra: "People don't have to do business with me, and so my best PR is doing everything within my power to assure they have the most memorable stay possible that specifically meets their needs and wants."

Three Points Within This Chapter Deserve Special Consideration

How Are the Most Successful Companies Making Sure They Offer an Ongoing and Constantly Improving Unique Value to Their Customers?

While there are debates out there and associated data that suggest that "trying too hard" does not garner the hoped-for results like loyal customers for a lifetime, we are still finding that **customers are four times more likely to leave a service disloyal than loyal.** Service (or the lack thereof) accounts for most of the "disloyalty pie." We tend to buy from a company because of the level of consistent quality products/services we receive from them, and we often leave a company because it fails to deliver on customer service.[2]

We must acknowledge that there are so many ways customers are being "served" by you today: **in person, through a delivery driver or call center worker and through email, chatbots, review sites, and, of course, social media.** So it isn't a surprise that, **in the United States, customer satisfaction ratings are at an all-time low according to the American Customer Satisfaction Index.**[3]

Paying attention to all of the access points for your customers, assessing their satisfaction, and then using the feedback will offer you the best opportunity to serve your customers with excellence through any medium. And sharing customer feedback appropriately is key as well. Too many organizations make the mistake of sharing customer feedback with only a certain subset of the employee group like the "customer service department" or the department whose function was being assessed. **Smart companies share customer feedback with all employees because it is as a collective team that allows you to provide optimal customer service**. You should be able to count on one another as partners to assure that your role is fulfilled with quality and care every time.

How Do Successful Companies Manage to Serve Their Eclectic Group of Customers With Consistent Excellence?

As mentioned earlier, your customers have numerous methods of interacting with you—a couple of which are more personal while others are greatly removed from direct interaction. Be glad for those opportunities where you are able to interact directly with your customers in person or by phone or personal email/text because those represent your greatest likelihood of providing service excellence. You have an exchange of communication that, because of the directness of contact, stands a greater opportunity for you to understand their needs/wants and for both parties to exchange thoughts, ultimately resulting in the customer being served based on their needs/wants.

Excellent communication should be your everyday goal, but it is fraught with challenge even on a good day. **Communication breaks down because there are (1) too many links in the chain, (2) undefined expectations, (3) failure to consider differences in communication skills/styles, (4) use of language/jargon, and (5) culture.**[1] Controlling your understanding of the needs/wants of the customer with whom you are having a more personal exchange is difficult enough. The customer communicating with you at large on social media, chatbots, review sites, and so on makes it almost impossible to eliminate the aforementioned challenges while putting your organization at risk for negative reviews for which you have little recourse because hundreds/thousands are reading the exchanges you and the complaining/requesting customer are having.

Take a little time with your experts to analyze how you are doing in interpersonal communication within your business. Explore with your customers what they appreciate and what they would like to see changed and then do the bravest thing—find two strategies that you will employ within your organization to change for the better. Once your direct interaction communication strategies are at their highest level, look at your secondary channels like review sites, social media, and chatbots. **How can you better assure that those customers can contact you directly for making their requests before they get to a point of broadcasting your perceived shortcomings online.**

And, perhaps **most importantly, serve whomever you are interacting with at the moment with excellence so that they are not just pleased but delighted.**

Does My Attitude Really Impact How the Customer Views My Performance as It Relates to Service Excellence?

We have all read and been lectured on the importance of having a positive attitude at work—being proud of the work you do and consistently displaying a desire to delight others. So, yes, **your attitude is THE KEY to how customers view your performance.** Even when you are not able to give the customer everything they want, they are far more likely to accept an alternative based on how you presented the information—with respect, good listening and responding, focusing on them and their issue, communicating understanding.

The key components of good customer service include (1) personalization, (2) empathy, (3) responsiveness, (4) product knowledge, and (5) professionalism.[4] These aforementioned elements make up your attitude and, bottom line, who you are. They should be at your fingertips at every interaction as you strive to deliver the best value possible.

Be proud of who you are every day and bring that feeling of accomplishment to your job regardless of what your functions may be or your level of empowerment. **You are worthy of being the owner and practitioner of the best service living out your own personal values.**

CHAPTER 5

Seek and Use Feedback

We all need people who will give us feedback. That's how we improve.

—Bill Gates, American Business Magnate

By midmorning the following day, Phil delivered the repaired car to Holly's home. Sergio paid for the surprisingly modest bill. It was way cheaper than he expected. He thanked Phil profusely and offered a substantial tip for the above and beyond service. Phil immediately and humbly declined the offer saying that they truly meant their company slogan—*We help by all means.* They truly live their mission.

After a hearty breakfast, the four thanked Holly and went on their way.

As they waved to Holly from a distance, Ava said, "I wouldn't mind staying there for a few more days. Holly really made us feel at home and special."

The men concurred.

The rest of the trip was uneventful, and, soon with Ava's guidance, they reached the summer villa.

The large villa looked imposing much like a castle in the woods. It was surrounded by a variety of tall trees. The bean shaped pool glowed in the sun's rays. A well-manicured lawn led to a nearby lake.

Sergio was impressed, "What a beautiful summer home you have, Ava."

Ava smiled,

Thank you. We spent most of our summers here as young children. We love nature, and this place has brought us so many happy memories. The house has enough bedrooms, so there was always plenty of space for us to have many friends and family members over. A trip here has become a family summer reunion. We're so happy the three of you can join us this summer.

Ray slowly got out of the car, "Thank you so much for inviting us over. This is such a lovely place. Looks like we'll have a lot of fun."

A warm friendly female voice filled the air, "Gentlemen, welcome. Hi, Dad, so good to see you! How was the trip? I heard you had an accident. Is everyone okay?" It was Liza, Glenn's daughter and Ava's mom. She has a busy career as a Vice-President for Customer Service for a major retail group. While she lived a hectic lifestyle, she made it a point to take some of the summer off every year. It was her personal time—spend time with family, enjoy nature, and get healthy. This year was even more special as she is ready to plan for the next steps in her life's journey.

Glenn stepped out of the car, "We're fine. It was just a minor car accident. And come to think of it, I'm glad we had it because we ended up in this amazing bed and breakfast."

Liza gave Glenn and Ava a big hug, "Great to see you guys. Glad you're all okay."

She turned to Sergio and Ray, "Sergio and Ray, great to finally meet both of you. Dad has told me so many stories about you. I've always felt you were part of our family. Welcome to our home!"

Ray shook her hand and gave her a hug, "Thank you so much for inviting us over. You have such a beautiful home!" Sergio echoed Ray's words and gave Liza a hug.

A handsome young man stepped out of the house to join the group.

Liza beckoned him over to join them in the driveway, "Ray, Sergio please meet my son Allan, Ava's twin."

Ray and Sergio shook Allan's hand.

"Well, look at that" Sergio said, "These two almost look like a replica of each other. What good looking young people!"

Glenn smiled, "Well they definitely got good genes from their grandfather!"

Everyone laughed.

Allan walked toward the back of the car, "You all must be tired. Let me get your bags and take you to your rooms."

Glenn walked over to give his grandson a hug and help him with the bags, " Thank you, Allan. As I got up earlier, my bones and muscles were making all sort of creaking sounds."

Allan laughed, "You look great, grandpa. We're so glad you and your friends are here."

Glenn winked at him, "Looks can be deceiving. I look forward to spending time with you this summer."

Allan gathered the bags, "Me too, grandpa."

Liza and Ava helped the gentlemen with their bags and led them into the house.

Liza smiled warmly and said, "Well, you must be hungry. I have cookies and lemonade ready. We can have a little snack and then I can show you around the house."

Ray looked through the window, "That would be great. I'm about ready for the pool!"

Glenn joined Ray, "Don't worry, buddy. We'll have lots of time to relax by the pool this summer. Liza, we'd like to cover the costs of our food and living expenses over the summer. We don't expect to stay free of charge."

Liza frowned at him, "Oh, dad. You are all part of our family. Please just enjoy my home because it is now yours as many times as you wish to visit. That includes all of you."

Glenn walked over and put his arms around her, "We insist on contributing something, dear, and will figure out how best to do that. Besides, you have no idea how much we eat and drink when we're together. I tell you, it would put a bear to shame."

They all laughed.

Sergio was curious, "Speaking of bears, are there any around here?"

Liza pointed to a site in the large yard, "We saw one over there three years ago. Never saw one again."

The gentlemen had their refreshments and soon after Liza took them on a guided tour of the home. The men were genuinely impressed by the Southern style décor and the welcoming nature of the home.

After the tour, Liza, Allan, and Ava proceeded to the kitchen to prepare a quick lunch for everyone.

The gentlemen took a walk around the beautiful garden in the front yard.

As a force of habit, Glenn surveyed the surroundings carefully.

"This is a fairly remote place, so I want to make sure we don't have any uninvited visitors" he said, " It's best to be safe." After scouting the surroundings, Glenn declared it all clear and suggested they sit by the pool.

The pool offered a breathtaking view of a forested area and the distant mountains.

The men took their seats for lunch.

Allan turned on the bug eliminating gadget and brought cold water for the gentlemen.

Ray turned his gaze to the nearby lake, "I heard there's good fishing in these parts."

Allan nodded,

For sure, the lake has bass, trout, catfish, bluegill, and crappie. Big ones too. I've had good luck fishing here during the summers. The grilled fish make awesome dinners too! Remember the big one you caught a few years back, grandpa?

Glenn smiled, "Oh, yes. I remember that one. If you didn't help me, I don't think I could have reeled it in. I think I still have the photo in my phone somewhere. I'll show you guys later."

Sergio was thrilled, "Fishing by the lake should really be exciting! I came prepared. Hopefully, I get to catch some big ones too."

Glenn looked to his right side then exclaimed, "Look, over there in the dark area by the tall trees."

They joined him and focused their gaze along the tall trees.

"Do you see those reddish colored eyes just by the tree line?" Glenn asked.

"I do" Ray said quietly. The others concurred.

"I believe those are coyotes. We need to be careful," Glenn said as he walked toward his small travel bag that contained a handgun.

"I hate shooting animals," Glenn continued, "But won't hesitate if it will protect us. They're probably just scoping us out to see who the new arrivals are."

Ray pulled out his binoculars and said,

You're right, those are most likely coyotes. They typically don't attack humans since they fear us as a result of experiences with hunters and ranchers. But, we should be careful in case they are hungry. They also tend to be territorial. We need to be careful about not leaving any food outside as well to draw them or any other animals to the cabin.

Sergio took photos using his cellphone, "They tend to follow proven trails and sometimes roads and shorelines of lakes. This house is probably near their trail. That's how they found us."

Allan gave the matter some thought and said, "We don't see them often. They must be very keen observers or picked up our scent when you all walked around the property."

Sergio nodded,

True, and they are day and night hunters, so they can be seeking food at any time. They are always on the hunt for an opportunistic meal! Much like in the business world and in careers, you need to *know your environment well and who you're up against.* With this knowledge you can take the best course of action. Your grandfather stressed the importance of scoping our new location even today in a place he knows well. Excellent reminder to always be aware of your surroundings.

Glenn nodded,

I guess I did. A career of doing so makes it natural for me to see to the safety and security of others and myself. Speaking of careers, how's your job search going, Allan? Still interested in a customer service position like your mom's?

Allan smiled, "I've been applying for jobs but don't have any interviews lined up yet. Yes, a corporate career in customer service would really be my dream job."

Glenn got his sunglasses from the small bag and said, "Well, we are full of experience in the customer service field so feel free to pick our brains this summer. We're always happy to offer advice!"

Allan was grateful, "I'd appreciate any help."

Ray had an idea,

One thought I have is to know yourself well enough to be able to "sell" the value you can provide to a potential employer or business. We spoke of scoping earlier. In business, one important benefit of scoping things out is to get some clarity on where the company stands as a business overall but also where you, yourself as an employee would stand within the company. You should start thinking about this early in the job search process.

Think about where you can make an important contribution to the company, which means researching every organization you are interested in working with before you ever send a resume. Remember, companies are driven to win and tend to be quite competitive. They benchmark their performance against competitors and industry leaders. That allows them to refine their strategies over time to remain the "best" in their field. Scope them out—their culture, values, goals, and how you might fit in helping their company keep winning. We "scope" a lot in my healthcare company. And, in my profession as a doctor, I like to constantly check on my ratings to understand what my patients think of my service and what I need to do to improve. But I've also learned that I'm *not just competing against other medical practices but with anyone that has served my patient in any way.* It sure broadens my field of consideration and competition!

Sergio agreed,

Yes, in practically any business organization, you need to check in with your customers as well as your competitors. And, as Ray said, the competition is not just in your direct field. In reality, it is any business that has served your customer well. You are now held to that standard and don't even know it!

In academia, the universities are ranked against each other according to various criteria, and the professors are rated by students on the courses they teach. Over the years, I have found the feedback helpful as a way of improving my craft and for planning any appropriate modifications of that course in the following semester. I also assess how purposeful my research is which guides such future endeavors.

Allan gave the matter some thought,

I think it's the same way for students too. In college, I learned the most from professors who give good feedback on projects and offer suggestions for improvement. I remember working on a business plan in one of my classes, the professor gave me a rough time. I felt like she was always making suggestions for improvement—nothing I did was ever good enough. I started off with a poor grade in class, but as I learned more and incorporated her suggestions, the plan improved dramatically. As a result of listening to feedback and acting on it, I ended up with an A in the class.

Sergio smiled,

Good for you! I wish all of my students were that way. *Getting feedback is one thing, but acting on the feedback is another.* The students I have seen succeed were willing to make the change. They had the confidence to keep seeking input no matter how challenging it appeared and the courage to make difficult changes even if it was cumbersome and inconvenient.

Ray chimed in,

I've noticed the same in business organizations. Executives who embrace change and master the art of change management tend to go up the corporate ladder. Companies that use feedback to improve their operations and customer relationships end up well rewarded.

Allan sipped on his water,

Nowadays, with social media, companies get almost instantaneous feedback on the quality of service they provide, and the data is easily available on the Web, so it can spread like wildfire, especially if a business gets bad reviews for service.

"Yes" said Sergio,

In our hotel business, we are well aware of the damage a very dissatisfied guest can do if they post adverse comments online, so there are two main things we do as a business. First, we encourage customers to tell us about anything they're not totally happy with during their stay, so we can rectify it immediately, and by the way, *we call these issues "opportunities" not "problems" or "complaints" as a great response to a poor customer experience will often enhance their loyalty.* Second, we are aware that customers who choose to post things on the Web are not necessarily giving us a comprehensive and representative view of the service we provide, so we do extensive and in-depth research with customers to identify where we can make small improvements at any point on the customer journey.

Glenn offered,

Before we head into lunch, Allan, I'd also suggest that the customer isn't always right, but they are your primary source of income and so listening to them carefully and balancing their input with that of others is critical for your continued success and that of your business. Customers have wants and needs. It's important for you to be able to analyze those and always strive to meet their needs at the very least.

Well, Allan I told you you'd get some good advice. More to come over the summer, we promise! By the way, it seems like the red eyes have disappeared guys. I guess they've concluded there are better prospects for a meal elsewhere, but don't worry, I'll keep a sharp lookout while we're here.

Allan stood up,

Thank you, gentlemen. Looks like I learned an important lesson about a career in service today. It's important to *know your terrain and gather constant feedback on your performance and, most importantly, use it to be better.* Everybody ready for lunch?

They all stood up and made a beeline toward the kitchen. They were more than ready to enjoy lunch.

Mastering Customer Service

Insight 5: Benchmark Against the Best Within and Outside Your Industry and Constantly Monitor Customers' Views of Your Level of Service

Seek and Use Feedback

We have said at the end of Chapter 2 that **understanding your customers' needs and priorities is the essential starting point for delivering excellent service. But, that's only the starting point. You then have to make sure, continuously, that you're meeting those needs and priorities and doing so at least as well and preferably better than other organizations. To do this, you have to get feedback from customers on how they feel about their experience** with your organization and use it, constantly, to improve.

Asking Customers for Feedback

In the Chapter 2, we explained qualitative research for understanding what's important to customers. To gather and use feedback necessitates quantitative research, which uses much larger samples to generate reliable data on how customers feel about their experience. Generating data based on larger samples is essential so that the statistics are sufficiently reliable to track movement over time and to compare with other organizations. **To be reliable, a sample has to be random, representative of the composition of the customer base, and sufficiently large.** The technical term for a random sample is a probability sample. Its key characteristic is that it is without bias because in a probability sample every customer stands an equal chance (probability) of ending up in the sample.[1]

The question of sample size is more complicated. It is reasonable to say that the accuracy of a sample is based on two things, the size of the sample and the amount of variance in the population to be surveyed. Size is straight forward and is based on the absolute size of the sample, not on what proportion of the population has been surveyed. A larger sample will always be more accurate than a smaller one,[2] regardless of the size of the customer base. Standard deviation is the normal measure of variance used to calculate the reliability of a sample size. The more variance there is, for example, differences in customers' views about the level of service provided, the larger the sample needs to be for a reliable result. Since standard deviations in customer satisfaction surveys are relatively low compared to most other types of surveys, a sample size of 200 can be considered sufficient for adequate reliability of customer experience monitoring.[3] The only caveat to this would be if an organization had many subgroups where it wanted to monitor customer service separately. For example, if Ray wanted to monitor and compare service quality in his health and wellness retail outlets, he would need a sample of at least 200 for each one. So, if the company had 50 retail stores, it would need a sample of at least 10,000 customers. And one final point, that's 10,000 responses not 10,000 surveys sent out.

Finally for sample reliability, if a sample is to provide a result that accurately reflects the views of the larger population of customers, it also has to be representative of that larger population. This is simple in principle. If females are 60 percent of the customer base, they should also be 60 percent of the sample. If over 65s are 17 percent of the customer base, they should be 17 percent of the sample, and so on for all segments. However, as we will see below it can be somewhat more complex depending on the type of survey undertaken.

While there are many possible methods for conducting a customer survey, the large majority of organizations will use either interviews or a self-completion survey. Interviews are more appropriate for organizations with a smaller customer base as response rates will be better, and this is important for generating a sample that is sufficiently large to be reliable. Interviews are ideal for ensuring that the sample is representative, as quotas can be set to ensure that, in the final sample, customer groups are represented in their correct proportions. To give a simple example, if 40 percent of your customers are male and the target sample size is 500, once 200 males have been interviewed, that quota is full, and no further males would be interviewed. Interviews can be conducted face to face or online using software such as Teams or Zoom, but telephone interviews would be the most common method for customer surveys.

Self-completion surveys are now most commonly online, but paper surveys have by no means died out, especially if they can be distributed personally to customers who visit the premises. Response rates for self-completion surveys are almost always lower and that reduces reliability since it introduces "nonresponse bias"; in other words, the minority of customers who choose to complete the survey may not have the same characteristics or opinions as the majority who don't.

Most self-completion surveys are now online, and if the software used is sophisticated enough, quotas can be set to ensure that the final sample is representative. If the software does not have that capability or if paper questionnaires are used, there is no control over how many customers from each segment complete the survey so the final sample will almost certainly not be representative. With sufficient expertise (which any research agency would possess for organizations that don't have it in-house), this can be corrected at the analysis stage by weighting the segments in their correct proportions.

Benchmarking

There are three main ways that you can compare your organization's performance at satisfying customers with the performance of other organizations. First, you can ask the customers; second, you can use published data; and third, you can conduct mystery shopping.

Ask the Customer.   **When you seek feedback from customers about how satisfied they are with your organization's performance, you should always include some questions about how you compare with others.** Many organizations are only interested in comparing against companies in their own sector. They say things like "*how can you compare a restaurant with an airline?*" The answer is that you can compare them in lots of ways and that's exactly what customers do. Taking the restaurant and airline as examples, both have websites, which may be easy or difficult to use. Customers wishing to self-serve on the

Web don't just compare you with direct competitors, they compare you with the best website they are in the habit of using and expect yours to be as good. To take a different element of customer service, the same would be true about telephone service. Factors such as time to get through, courtesy, knowledge, and empowerment of the advisor are comparable across all organizations from any sector. So, if the customer transacted via the website, the question might be *"how easy did you find it to use the XYZ Inc website compared with any other websites that you have used recently?"*

Use Published Data. There are usually published sources of data that enable you to compare your levels of customer satisfaction against many other organizations. For example, in the United States, there is the American Customer Satisfaction Index (ACSI)[4] published by the University of Michigan, and in the United Kingdom, there is the United Kingdom Customer Satisfaction Index (UKCSI)[5] published by the Institute of Customer Service. If you want to compare the satisfaction levels of your customers against the best on those published league tables, you need to make sure that at least a part of your survey uses a comparable methodology. For example, if their customer satisfaction is rated on a 10-point numerical scale and their headline measure is a composite index (as both the ACSI and the UKCSI are), yours needs to be the same.

Mystery Shopping. Some organizations view mystery shoppers as customer substitutes. True, they have to go through a typical customer journey. If they're mystery shopping a hotel, they will stay overnight, eat dinner and breakfast, and use any other facilities such as a health club. But are they the same as real customers? Of course they're not. Professional mystery shoppers are exactly that. They are highly trained to observe and record many detailed aspects of the service delivery process and consequently provide highly detailed information that is very useful to operational managers. Examples might include whether the hotel receptionist was wearing a name badge, addressed the customer by name, and provided clear directions to the room. They can record waiting times at check-in and check-out as well as in the restaurant. They can also make judgments on levels of cleanliness or staff friendliness and helpfulness. Technology even permits surreptitious video recording of staff, though companies need to think carefully about the implications of this for organizational culture and values.[6] **So, mystery shopping provides many practical benefits for operational managers for use in staff training, evaluation, and recognition but can't provide understanding of how customers feel about the customer experience and the attitudes they are forming about the company.**

Since mystery shoppers' profession is to make observations on companies' customer service performance, they cease to be normal customers, becoming highly aware and often much more critical than typical customers.[7] While this is good for their role, it doesn't provide an accurate reflection of how normal customers feel.[8] Morrison et al. reported other inconsistencies with mystery shopping, such as males and older people producing less accurate reports than females or younger ones.[9]

Smile School.   In their book "Loyalty Myths," Keiningham et al. use the experience of Safeway in America to illustrate the dangers of mystery shopping.[6] They explain how Safeway based its strategy in the 1990s on delivering superior customer service and invested in an extensive mystery shopping program to monitor employees' performance in delivering it. Employees were expected to do things like thank customers by name, offer to carry their groceries to the car, smile, and make eye contact: all very desirable customer service behaviors which should lead to customer satisfaction. And they did. Throughout the 1990s, Safeway's customer satisfaction levels and financial returns were very high. However, in stark contrast to the teachings of the Service-Profit Chain,[10] customer satisfaction and employee satisfaction were moving in opposite directions. This was because employees who failed to achieve a target mystery shopping score were sent for remedial training (called Smile School by the employees) and could be dismissed if their performance failed to improve. Moreover, female employees' feeling that the smiling and eye contact could send the wrong signals to some male shoppers was confirmed by an increase in the number of sexual harassment incidents committed by customers. This led to a number of charges filed against Safeway by the employees' union and some individual female employees. In the end, the Service-Profit Chain wasn't wrong. Poor employee morale adversely affected customer satisfaction and Safeway's financial performance. According to the ACSI,[4] Safeway's customer satisfaction levels rose substantially from 70 percent to a high of 78 percent by 2000 as a result of its focus on customer service. However, as problems with employees intensified, the customer satisfaction gains were virtually all lost, with Safeway's score falling back to 71 percent by 2003.

It is increasingly recognized by good employers that mystery shopping is best used for factual rather than judgmental aspects of service and to provide positive feedback and recognition to employees. **Good companies also understand that it provides operational information rather than a reliable measure of how satisfied or dissatisfied customers feel.**

CHAPTER 6

Reinvent Yourself Constantly

Always render more and better service than is expected of you, no matter what your task may be.

—Og Mandino, American writer

"Reel it in!" Glenn yelled at Ray excitedly.

"I got it … I got it … I think it's a big one." Ray said, as the others looked on.

Ray struggled a little bit, and his heavy and abrupt movements rocked the aluminum jon boat. They all held on to the side of the boat to steady themselves.

"Whoa … Whoa!" Sergio exclaimed, concerned they might topple over.

Luck, skill, and diligence converged, and Ray reeled in the first catch of the expedition—a 20-in. bass. He posed with his catch as Sergio and Allan took photos, then unhooked the fish returning it to the water. The fish swam away with a large splash.

It was now 10:30 a.m., they had ventured out on the boat around 9:00 a.m., right after having coffee and cereal for breakfast.

During the first hour, the quartet enjoyed the beauty and solitude of the lake. The rays of the early morning sun made the water sparkle. The mountains and lush trees served as an equally beautiful backdrop.

They didn't have much luck during the first hour. But then, Ray brought in the first catch and excitement built from there.

Right after Ray released the fish, everyone relaxed and drank their bottled water. It seemed like a perfect time for a brief pause.

Sergio breathed in deeply, "Isn't this lake breeze amazing?"

Glenn sipped on his water and nodded, "Truly relaxing. I feel younger already," he said jokingly.

Sergio smiled, "I think it would take more than that for me."

Everyone laughed.

"Not sure, all this will change our chronological age. But, hey, if it makes us feel younger, then it's all good." Ray said.

"Speaking of trying to be younger, Sergio, I notice you've lost a lot of weight since I last saw you. 50–60 pounds? You look great—a lot more buff," Glenn joked.

Sergio smiled shyly.

Thanks, I gained a lot of weight over the years, and my daughter has been pushing me to get healthier. So I started a regimen of eating less and focusing on more healthy foods along with an enhanced exercise routine. The next thing I knew, I felt physically, mentally, and emotionally better and was soon able to do things I hadn't done in years. I became a lot more active and had much more energy. It was quite transformative!

"Good for you," Glenn said admiringly, "That takes a lot of willpower and discipline."

Sergio took a sip of water,

I guess there comes a time in one's life when we commit to make drastic changes to get to a better place. I knew in my academic career, I had to *constantly re-create a new version of myself to stay relevant in my field. Rather than being content with the management theories I had grown comfortable with, I made an effort to learn more about technologies and then developed new concepts and ideas by blending both.*

Allan munched on a protein bar and said,

One of my professors in college did a similar thing. She was a traditional, art history professor, and she made an effort to learn about digital art creation and blended her knowledge of the old and the new. I had a fun class with her. At first she struggled with the technology but later made it work. It ended up as an awesome class.

Sergio put his cap on to avoid the glaring sun,

That's impressive. I'm sure the process wasn't easy for her. She had to dig deep, reframe the way she learned, and reinvent the way she did things. That was quite tough. But *pride in her work, discipline, and the drive to learn at the end of the day made a huge difference* for her students.

Glenn commented,

I read once that *we are all "icebergs." Others see of us what is above the water—our appearance and behaviors but don't really know what is beneath the water—what drives us to do what we do: our personality, experiences, values.* I believe that is why some people can make those critical changes to stay with the game and even ahead, while others simply cannot. Achieving ongoing success is very dependent on our "iceberg" characteristics.

Ray checked on his slightly tangled fishing line and added,

Glenn, you are so right. You know, a lot of artists and business leaders have reinvented themselves to find new levels of success. Madonna continued to stay relevant in the industry for years through reinvention. In the 1800s, American Express predominantly offered express mail and transportation of valuable goods. Then, they expanded their offering to include traveler's checks and money orders. In the mid-1900s, they reinvented themselves again by offering a card extending credit to customers and businesses. As we can see today, that reinvention led to their being dominant in the field of finance and service for nearly two centuries.

Glenn picked up his fishing rod,

As you all know, I did quite a reinvention on the personal front. Rather than building a career in engineering, which was my natural first love, I became a military officer. I wasn't sure I would use my engineering degree as I might have done in the private sector, but looking back, I realize that I used those skills in several ways throughout my military career. And what I learned in the military has allowed me to pursue a variety of interests both career-wise and as hobbies after retirement. I know so many retired military personnel who have joined a private company or started their own business and are doing very well.

"Could reinvention be essential for success in the service field as well?" Allan wondered.

Sergio was quick to reply,

Definitely. I sometimes talk about the case of Chipotle Mexican Grill in my classes. Prepandemic, they served their customers using a walk-in, counter service approach where customers select custom order food items. When the pandemic happened, they shifted their model to please customers in a new way and improve safety protocols for their customers and staff. They introduced drive-thru pick up lanes designed for orders by mobile phone. With this reinvention, they were able to quickly attend to the needs of more customers. This move also improved their service quality and kept them in business during a very trying time.

Allan agreed,

That is very true. Amazon does a lot of innovation and reinvention too. I remember reading a quote from Jeff Bezos not too long ago. It was something about customers are like invited guests to a party, and Amazon is the host. The company's job is to make the customer experience a little better every single day.

Sergio smiled, "Sounds like constant reinvention to me. Given the volume of customers they have worldwide, they must be doing something right."

Allan nodded, "I suppose *with the popularity of remote work, many companies out there are reinventing their business models and concepts of service as well.*"

Sergio adjusted his cap,

For sure. And, not just companies, but workers too! In academia, during Covid, professors and all in the teaching profession had to quickly learn new tools to be able to teach online. Many of us did it for the first time during the pandemic and are still perfecting it to this day as remote learning continues in some settings.

Ray put his bait on and added,

Some of the doctors I know stayed in telehealth and telemedicine even after the original pandemic had ended. It was a shift from the traditional way of treating patients, but they realized they were able to broaden their geographic reach and serve patients in new ways, and the patients appreciated the flexibility as well.

"My brother is a perfect example of the benefit of reinvention," Glenn added.

He was passionate about cars and serving his customers but had no interest at all in technology. He was one of the last people I know to get a mobile phone. But as cars incorporated more microchips, he had no choice but to master all the new technology, and before long, he embraced it so much that he's now its biggest advocate. His customers all have an app on their phone that manages every aspect of car ownership for them. It holds records of every transaction, so they have a complete history without keeping any files. It tracks any financial transaction about servicing, insurance, and taxes and keeps them informed about essential matters such as new legislation. So, his customers get a superior value proposition, which, in turn, has enhanced their loyalty.

Allan cast his fishing line into the water, "Didn't he win a technology award a few years back?"

Glenn laughed,

He did! It was a technology innovation award in the auto industry. It's amazing how he transformed himself and his company from a laggard to industry leader. It took a lot of time, effort, and investment, but he made it happen. He clearly had the "iceberg" characteristics to make all of this happen and capitalized on it. He also managed to support and guide his employees and partners to make the change. There was a lot of resistance at first. It was, after all, a drastic change, but somehow it worked. He was driven to make things easier and better for all his customers. And from what I've been reading, similar shifts are happening in many industries as well, and the *companies that are thriving are the ones who have adapted and reconfigured their operations to suit the new environment and meet the new demands of customers.*

Allan tugged on his line, but there was nothing,

I've heard of several similar company stories, grandpa. Companies that found a new way of doing things and their business just took off. Some startups in our university even reinvented a business model to serve customers in a new way. The results have been promising, and I heard some of them are doing well.

Glenn cast his line in the water, "It's amazing what a healthy dose of reinvention can do."

Allan speculated,

Interesting new world we're living in. One can only imagine how else service careers and corporate service offerings will change a decade or so from now. What else will be reinvented? Based on what has transpired in recent years, it looks like there will continue to be a lot of reinventions in the future.

Sergio didn't have much luck with his fishing line, "I'm not having much luck. Who knows, maybe fishing will get reinvented in the future too!"

Mastering Customer Service

Insight 6: Be Prepared to Reinvent Yourself Constantly

Reinventing Yourself Constantly

Sergio reminds us that he had to constantly re-create a new version of himself to stay relevant in his field. Rather than being content with the management theories he had grown comfortable with, he made an effort to learn more about technologies and then developed new concepts and ideas by blending both. This takes an **earnest review of how you are doing business, how the world is changing, being open to finding the best changes for you, and making them**.

Allan comments about a professor he had that was not at all comfortable with technology changes in her field, but her **pride in her work, discipline, and the drive to keep learning** at the end of the day propelled her to pursue needed changes, and she remains devoted to reinventing herself everyday both for her and her students.

Reinvention is not easy nor comfortable. We must commit to an attitude of constant improvement and realize that we will **never "arrive."** We will never be the best, know it all, nor have the perfect approach for everything despite our knowledge, experience, and education. Opening ourselves up to be a little better every day in some fashion makes us a role model for others who are striving to create their niche both in their careers and personal lives. Because once we decide to be better every day, it impacts us in all aspects of our lives. While that might frustrate people whose personal tendencies aren't supportive of constant change, it is the best thing for you and those around you. Be your best self always!

Three Points Within This Chapter Deserve Special Consideration

Why Is Reinvention Important to You and Your Business/Career?

Because the experience you create with your customer is the main differentiator between you and your competitors. If you want to stay in business, you will have to reinvent and improve customer experiences with every interaction because your competitors are doing exactly that. And remember, your **competitors are every company that your**

customer is doing business with—not just within your field. Your challenges are huge!

Part of why you are in business is to assure you stay in business. According to Bain and Company, **increasing customer retention rates by just 5 percent can increase profits by between 25 and 95 percent! And investing in new customers is between 5 and 25 times more expensive than retaining existing ones.** It has been found that **businesses can grow revenues between 4 and 8 percent above their market when prioritizing better customer service experiences.**[1]

Certainly, a company that improves itself constantly to assure that they provide excellent customer service has a team that does more than answer questions and solve customer issues. They go above and beyond with each interaction to continue to attract that customer's loyalty. So, setting a standard within your organization of excellent service with every customer contact takes work—lots of it and yet too many companies are reluctant to invest money on customer service assessments/education/follow through because it isn't viewed as a money-maker or likely to increase your new customer base. Statistics prove that it is **more profitable to pour effort into retaining existing customers in the long run with 20 percent of your current customers accounting for 80 percent of your company's profits!**[2]

Clearly, investing in improving yourself and your business constantly pays off for everyone—customers, employees, and the business. Plus, you are living values that you cherish! Companies that are thriving are the ones who have adapted and reconfigured their operations to suit the new environment and meet the ever-changing demands of customers.

Does Our Company Have to Jump on Board With Every Change That Is Happening in Our World Today?

The answer is "yes" and "no"! Your marketing and business departments must be watching advances on the horizon that may impact your field of work. Some of them may only be preliminary and in early discussion stages, but, as you painfully know, those **ideas can move at warp speed and be picked up by your competitors quickly so that they become the leaders in new approaches to products and service.** The analysis is simple then—they lead, you follow. Choose to be a leader in advancing your company strategically but constantly.

A real-life and recent example of unexpected but dramatic business process change is when the Covid-19 pandemic pushed us, in a moment's notice, to remote work in order to retain any semblance of business functioning. **Postpandemic, the popularity of remote work has remained,** and employees are now expecting and enjoying that privilege in many companies. While some functions must be done "in-house," every company—large and small—has found itself **reinventing their business models and concepts of service to stay ahead of the game, retain their employees, and use their skills well to better serve the customers**. Remote work is our new world!

Also, before the pandemic, businesses were taking their time in exploring new, digital ways to engage and serve customers. Again, with the pandemic and in a moment's notice, all of that changed. **Social media, live chat, video calls/meetings, and so on became the way we did business**. Yet we find, several years after the pandemic ended, that **only 50 percent of companies have enabled their teams with basic computer support systems, such as help desks, shared email/ file capabilities, education, and so on,** so that the services customers now expect can be provided seamlessly. Those businesses who have not kept up with the new communication methods find themselves playing catch-up every day to compete with the companies that are providing the aforementioned tools for their employees, which allows customers to be served in the way in which they have now become accustomed.[2] Assess and grow so that you can retain and attract customers with the new ways of doing business.

What Do Our Own Personality/Values/Experiences Have to Do With Service?

The **drivers of human behavior explain why we "show up" as we do.** We have mentioned before the iceberg concept—there is a "small" part that we see above the water but so much more under the water we don't even consider. The "public" portion above the water includes our appearance and behavior, and we are very good at judging people based on those two things through our own paradigm really knowing very little about the individual.

To fully appreciate someone, we have to go below the surface and attempt to understand as much as appropriate and possible about the "why's" of their behavior. That represents a dive into the "private" portion below the water and allows a better picture of their attitudes driven by needs, personality, values, and knowledge. Those are the things that drive us to do what we do.

Behaviors are driven by our attitudes toward people, places, and things. The stronger the attitude, the more consistent the behavior. Former smokers will tell us that their aversion to being in the presence of smoke is so strong that they will risk being viewed as rude to move away from that smell/exposure. On the other hand, many of us have lost and gained the same 20 pounds over and over because our attitude toward weight loss isn't as strong and we vacillate in our practices on any given day.

Attitudes Are Developed Based on Four Primary Factors

1. **Needs: Innate** (those we are born with like the need for food, warmth, touch) **and Acquired** (examples include the need for esteem, affiliation, achievement, and power).
2. **Personality: A combination of psychological traits that describe a person and influence behavior.** Personality preferences typically include extraversion/introversion, sensing/intuition, thinking/feeling, and judging/perceiving.
3. **Values: The central truths, laws, or beliefs from which arise the social rules of conduct.** Examples include respect, honesty, trust, and integrity.
4. **Knowledge: Is gained in the process of doing and experiencing things.**[3]

All of these elements are present in each one of us as human beings. On any given day, some of these characteristics are more prevalent than on other days. **Your job is to realize and appreciate who you are–your needs, personality characteristics, values and knowledge all of**

which you control and influence and use these assets on your behalf and that of your customers. While embracing and loving yourself is important, as a customer service professional, complementing your wants and needs with the customer's creates winners all around! That is your job! **Take a deep dive below the surface to assess who you are and, to the extent possible, who your customer is to assure the most positive and productive relationship.** Everyone wins!

CHAPTER 7

Collaborate While Maintaining Ownership

Teamwork is the ability to work together toward a common vision. The ability to direct individual accomplishment toward organizational objectives. It is the fuel that allows common people to attain uncommon results.

—Andrew Carnegie, American Industrialist

One evening, the group decided to start a campfire in the backyard. There was a large firepit surrounded by a dozen lounge chairs. Nearby was a gazebo that housed a wet bar with stools. On one side of the gazebo was a large commercial sized grill.

The plan for the night was to grill some hotdogs and burgers for dinner.

Allan passed around cold drinks, while Ava got the grill started.

Liza brought out a tray containing assorted vegetables, crackers, and cheese.

Sergio and Ray assisted Ava with the hotdogs and burgers.

Glenn sat on the far end away from the others. He was checking on his phone while occasionally glancing at the tall trees. He wanted to make sure there were no coyotes or any other wild animals nearby.

Liza brought him a glass of cold water and sat beside him, "I'm so glad you can join us this year, dad."

Glenn smiled, "Well, my dear, I'm retired. You may have to get used to the idea of seeing me more often."

Liza adjusted her seat, "That would really be a welcome change. I've missed not seeing you more and with the kids being gone soon to pursue their own lives, I could use some company. I always enjoy time with you."

Glenn put on some bug repellant and passed it to Liza, "You got it. I'll be around. By the way, how's work?"

Liza frowned,

I don't know, dad. I may be bored. As you know, I've done well and really moved up the corporate ladder. I've enjoyed my job and its unique challenges over the years, but at this stage, I feel like I want to do something else with my life. My job doesn't excite me the way it used to.

Glenn was surprised,

Hmmm. I didn't expect that to come from you. I always thought you enjoyed your job. After all, you do very important work. You set the tone, agenda, and direction for customer service for your company. In fact, your work impacts the lives of many customers and their well-being. You make a huge contribution toward the success of your company.

Liza nodded,

I believe that—that's exactly why I sometimes feel conflicted. I feel honored and privileged to help so many people. I just sometimes wonder if I could do even more in the next and possibly last 20 years of my career. I'm just wondering if I could transfer what I've learned in the corporate world and apply it in our government or perhaps an international nonprofit organization.

Glenn was pensive,

Liza, our government and nonprofit organizations would definitely benefit from your know-how. There is much room for improvement in service delivery in these sectors. You've always made the right choices and decisions throughout your career. This one is not any different. Follow what your heart tells you.

Liza looked at him, "I'm just not sure. I'm a little confused."

Glenn sipped on his water and said, "Don't worry. You'll do just fine. You'll come up with the right decision. You always do."

And your children, Liza, are wonderful! It's interesting but not surprising to see that both of them have decided to follow in your footsteps in the field of service. Ava in a service career and Allan in corporate customer service. It looks like Allan wants to be in a career like your current one, and Ava wants to be in a career you're thinking of moving into. You taught them well. They are respectful and focused people. Job well done, mom.

Liza glowed with the compliment, "Thank you, dad. The truth is I learned a few things about service from you too!"

Glenn laughed.

Liza continued,

Aside from caring about others and striving to make the world a better place, I also wanted the kids to learn about discipline just like in the military. I emphasized to them the need to *always be responsible and to be accountable for their actions.*

Glenn took another sip of water,

Well, it looks like you built that in their character as well. From what I heard about their work in college and their leadership roles in extracurricular activities, they both don't shy away from responsibilities. They'll have wonderful careers and lives, just like you.

"I hope so, dad." Liza said.

Glenn was confident,

I'm sure they will. Now, regarding the career change you're thinking about, you can spend the summer thinking about it. I remember in the past, you've spent this kind of time off coming up with amazing corporate strategies. Now is the time to concentrate just on you—what a change, right? You are a good planner. It's just part of who you are. So, simple as it sounds, *take the time to review the goals that got you to where you are today. Which of those still work for you and which ones are you feeling the need to let go.* Consider what you want to accomplish before you retire at the end of your current career (wherever that takes you next). *Set goals based on those dream accomplishments and get started!* Whatever you choose to do next will be a gift to the world, and I am so proud of you! You have always known that because your duties had a focus on customer service, that, in reality, customer service is everyone's job with every interaction and didn't just belong to the 'customer service department'. Your attitude of spreading the opportunities and responsibilities for providing service excellence throughout your company is just one of the reasons it is as successful today as it is!

Liza smiled, "You're right, dad. Now is the right time for me to plan a new future. Thanks for the encouragement and enlightenment. You are always the best guide I've ever had!"

Glenn patted her back, "You are my joy, and I'll always be there for you. I'm full of advice as you know well, but I'm a good listener too. You just let me know what you need at any time."

Just as their conversation ended, the others joined them. Ava and Allan brought drinks, and Sergio and Ray brought the hotdogs and burgers.

Ray started passing around food, "Time to get the party started!"

Just as Glenn was about to receive his hotdog, his phone rang. It was an unfamiliar number.

"Excuse me," he said looking at Ray, "Let me just take this call."

"Glenn Thompson, good evening" Glenn said, wondering who would be calling him at this time of night.

He smiled instantly recognizing a familiar voice,

How are you, Ambassador? Good to hear from you…. Certainly…. Not a problem…. I'll text you his name and number after we get off the phone.... How's Italy? It must be quite late there.... I now remember you hardly sleep.... Good to hear from you.... Not a problem at all. I'll take care of it. I'm on a fishing trip with old friends and family. When can you and I catch up?.... OK, great. I'll see you when you return to the States. Take care.

Glenn explained, "An old friend—Ambassador Jones. We go back a long way."

As promised, Glenn then sent a text from his phone to the Ambassador and continued,

He just misplaced the number of a mutual friend.... It's always nice to hear from old acquaintances. As a military officer, I collaborated with so many people from all walks of life, including the diplomatic community. Over the years, I've developed a lot of strong friendships and symbiotic relationships. *Many of my greatest successes happened as a result of collaboration with others.*

Ray took a bite on his hotdog and said,

I had similar experiences in my medical practice and business. I had opportunities every day to work with others and was able to achieve things faster and, many times, better because we all brought something unique to the table. I only have a specialty in one medical field, so when I came across complicated cases, I always approached other practitioners with different skills to collaborate and see things from a variety of perspectives.

Working with all of our brains, different experiences, and, potentially, different but appropriate approaches to best serve the needs of the patient is the absolute of service excellence. In building the company I founded, I knew that *to provide great service and keep our customers loyal, I would have to instill a culture of teamwork throughout the business.* Our frontline staff have great relationships with customers while realizing that their expertise is in service and not health and wellness. They link customers with appropriate health and wellness specialists but maintain their interest and involvement with their customers making regular courtesy calls to check progress and identify if their customers need any more help.

Sergio joined the conversation.

I agree with you there, Ray. As a customer, it can be very frustrating when frontline customer service staff hand you over to a specialist, thinking they've done their job and lose interest moving on to the next person to serve. If the health and wellness specialist in your example is unable to help or that relationship just doesn't work for the customer, you are left in limbo and have to start the process all over again. At the hotel chain where I serve on the Board, we are very conscious of that and make sure that *someone always owns the end-to-end customer experience.*

Glenn shared,

We join teams for a variety of reasons, including some that are more personal like security in numbers and a boost in self-esteem to have partners that understand your world. But most importantly, we have teams because of the sharing component that makes service really work for everyone.

Ava's eyes lit up as she came upon a realization,

As a student, my group projects in some classes were hit and miss. When I had conscientious teammates, we came up with high-quality work, but, in cases where we had ill-prepared or less committed group partners, our work turned out far less stellar. I guess in service careers and in corporate service offerings, *finding the right partners, who have the right skills and share your level of commitment and motivation, is essential.*

Sometimes, hard as you try, you can't make up for lack of quality work on the part of your teammates. Lesson learned—*always be a good partner, and, hopefully, you will encourage that behavior in others.*

Allan nodded,

I couldn't agree more, Ava. I've made mistakes in picking the wrong project teams when I first started college. I just thought everyone would come to the table with the same commitment that I had—not true! By my junior and senior years, I learned to carefully choose who to collaborate with, and in doing so, my projects were always in the A level. We worked hard, but with everyone putting in similar efforts, we achieved what we wanted. *Working with a talented and committed team that shares your passion toward a goal makes all the difference.*

Ray smiled, "Glenn, you must be so proud. You have very sharp grandchildren."
Glenn moved his grilling skewer closer to the fire,

I know. In fact, I have known that for quite some time. They learned so much from their mother. I can't wait to see what they will do after college. Hopefully, they could learn a few more tips from three old men this summer—before they embark on their careers.

Ava was quick to respond,

Correction—not three old men! Three very accomplished, energetic, and wise men. I keep thinking, how many of my friends and Allan's would have the privilege of spending time and gaining wisdom from people who have reached the pinnacle of their careers and are willing to share those insights with us? We're loving every minute of this trip and all of you!" "Here, here," Allan echoed.

Mastering Customer Service

Insight 7: *Collaborate With Others but Keep Ownership of the End-to-End Customer Experience*

Collaborate While Maintaining Ownership

Through the careers of Liza, Glenn, Ray, and Sergio and in the recent college experiences of Ava and Allan, we receive many insights regarding the power of teamwork yet maintaining ownership of the end-to-end process for our customer. Ava discusses learning to be responsible and accountable in group projects while in college and the difference it made in the quality of the outcome, while Allan commented on the impact a talented and committed team makes that also shares your passion for the topic and the positive product.

Ray reminds us that, particularly in medicine, it is critical to collaborate with others who have expertise that you don't have creating the likely best outcome for the patient. No egos welcome here!

For some people who have fought their way to where they are in their career, it can be very **difficult to let go of singular pride of accomplishment** and realize that as well-educated as you are, as well-experienced as you are, as knowledgeable as you are, you don't know it all and never will! We all benefit from the **Johari Window** that is a technique designed to help people better understand their relationship with themselves and others. It emphasizes:

- **OPEN Area: Things you know about yourself.**
- **BLIND Area: Things you don't know about yourself but others do.**
- **HIDDEN Area: Things you know about yourself but hide from others.**
- **UNKNOWN Area: Things that are unknown to you and to others about you.**[1]

We all have skills built over time and through a variety of sources, but we also have BLIND and UNKNOWN facets of our personalities which can impede possibilities in all aspects of our lives—definitely at work. If acknowledged and used, those might be an asset to our customer service approach. Appropriately engaging teamwork allows us to see (if we are OPEN) our best traits (HIDDEN or UNKNOWN) and those that could use some work.

As we work on being a good team member, always keep in mind that **your best day is yet to come, and the better version of yourself remains pliable.** Give yourself the opportunity to seek input on how you might be a better team member, which will only heighten your worth (personally and professionally).

Three Points Within This Chapter Deserve Special Consideration

Why Do I Have to Be the Only One Holding Myself Accountable and Responsible for My Actions?

We have all likely felt this frustration at some point in our careers. Going back to the Johari Window may provide us with some insights into why we feel this way and what we can do about it. **Some questions to ask yourself when you get the feeling that you are the only one putting forth the effort required to have the best outcome for the customer:**

1. Do you perhaps **enjoy a little too much the authority/power** you have with the team based on your title, experience, education? That might be a deterrent to others jumping in to assist/partner with you on the effort. They may not feel comfortable holding themselves accountable and responsible at a higher level, given their perception of needing your "permission" to move ahead.

2. Are you **open to input on what you do well and what could improve and do you seek and use that input?** If you don't appear receptive to feedback and have a higher level of authority/power (perceived or real) on the team, people are far less likely to share their thoughts with you about you leaving you BLIND.

3. Are you willing to do a **deep dive assessment of yourself and find your HIDDEN traits** that might actually benefit you and

the team if brought to light? Granted this takes introspection and courage, but certainly, you and the team could grow through your willingness to assess what you could do that you haven't in the past.

4. Are you open to realizing that **there are things you just don't know** or do well that others might? This is the true power of a team and the key to customer service excellence. Capitalize on what others bring to the table that is outside your expertise, experience, and knowledge.

In reality, when we feel that we are the only one being held accountable and responsible (by ourselves or others), we may have inadvertently created that "box" ourselves. **Be brave and assess how you can open more doors to make you a better team member** and see if that doesn't inspire others to do the same for themselves and to share more comfortably with you how you could bring greater value to the team.

Respect your teammates by supporting the sharing of talents, commitment, and passion toward an agreed-upon goal. Granted, sometimes we are given our team instead of choosing them. Do your best to **nurture partnerships and the right skills in yourself and others to achieve a mutually sought outcome. Collaboration = success**.

When Is the Right Time to Assess a Career Change That Means New Teams, Lots of Learning, Refocus?

There are certainly generational, ethnic, social, and family differences that impact when/if we change jobs, let alone careers. But, the **bottom line is that all of us have needs and wants. Some we don't acknowledge (per the Johari Window concepts), but they nudge at us subconsciously** at the very least, making us less comfortable with our current career/job even if we don't exactly know why we feel that way.

It's more than just setting life goals. While those are critically important so that you have some kind of roadmap for where you want to go and maybe even a loose timeline, if you are **ignoring some of**

your wants/needs, a goal document will still not bring you ultimate satisfaction.

As we have mentioned earlier, we all have needs, some innate and so natural we don't even think about them and others **acquired which include the need for esteem, affiliation, achievement and power**.[2] If you have a **need for esteem—feeling good about yourself and respected by others**—and your current employer isn't meeting that need, you may need to seek another job within that company or outside because your current situation isn't fulfilling for you.

Or do you have a **need for affiliation—to belong with an emphasis on social relationships**—and your current position is more isolated and stifling? You may need to move on.

Is the **need for achievement** high on your list of priorities (but perhaps BLIND to you)? People with this need are **motivated by winning and rewards. They love to solve problems**. If your current role doesn't allow you these opportunities, you may need to look elsewhere within the organization or outside to better fulfill your personal requirements.

Finally, if you have a **need for power—to be in control**—you may wish to be self-employed because, in reality, what any of us controls in our lives particularly professionally is very small. Our world is an interactive and team-oriented one that requires us to be supportive and cooperative in achieving goals, especially corporate ones. Even with pursuing and achieving our personal goals, we need others to assist us along the way. Be kind to yourself and work out why you need control, address those issues, and lighten your burden because no job will ever fit your expectations of control. Remember that **the uncompromising person is most always alone**.

Now the key is **taking the time to analyze yourself—your needs and wants** based on the aforementioned categories. Be honest as it is just you talking to you about you. Perhaps growing up, you had a less than supportive and nurturing household. It has left you with self-esteem issues. Taking a job and "hoping" to enjoy it is not a strategy that often wins for you or your customers. If you are an outgoing person and enjoy being around others with constant interactions, you will likely not flourish in a job where there is significant isolation. If you truly enjoy growing and learning, then you may have the need for achievement and finding the right company and job that encourages and facilitates those opportunities is probably best for you. And we've discussed the need for power above already—it is typically not a healthy characteristic for any us.

Every person likely has some or all of the aforementioned needs, but, often, one is more primary. That is the one to address as you are assessing whether to move to a new job or, certainly, a new career.

Remember too that your **"wants" may not always mirror your "needs,"** and thus, our advice for you to differentiate the two and focus on what your inner self is saying about your needs. You and your customers will always win with this kind of awareness and openness.

Are Teams Realistic and Necessary in This New Virtual World?

Rarely does anyone succeed without the assistance of others whether those people are family, friends, co-workers, educators, or, even, strangers. **Even the best and brightest do not live, work nor prosper in a vacuum**. Interdependency is a fact of our lives and one we would be wise to embrace for none of us know it all, regardless of our education and life experiences.

Working with the positive and supportive attitudes of those around you and taking advantage of their brain power, different experiences and likely different but appropriate approaches to best serve the needs of the customer is the absolute of service excellence. Plus, it **takes the burden off of you to be "perfect."**

That means **instilling a culture of teamwork throughout the business and, as an individual player on the team, enthusiastically joining in**. And when you are on teams (and there will be several going at any given time—at home and at work), **work together to assure that someone always owns the end-to-end customer experience**. As customers, we have all become frustrated when we are handed off to others within the business, which forces us to start all over with our request. Too rarely do we have a "go to" person within an organization that we can ask a question of and actually get a response back from that person, regardless of the nature of the issue. If you want to **differentiate yourself and your business from most others, create, support, and actively participate in assuring the customer has someone in the company that owns the end-to-end process for them.** That is the epitome of teamwork!

Yes, we **join teams for a variety of reasons, including some that are personal like security in numbers and a boost in self-esteem** to have partners that understand our world. But, **most importantly, we have teams because the sharing component makes service the best it can be for everyone**.

Let's call attention to the **difference between a "group" and a "team." A group can be defined as two or more people who come together for a common purpose.** That may sound like the definition of a team as well? Let's consider an example: You go to a movie theater to see a new film with a friend. There are 50 other people in the theater with you most of whom you likely don't know, but you are a "group" who have come together for a common purpose—to see the film. But you aren't a team.

Now, the local high school basketball team in action is not only a group who have come together for a common purpose but they also have the **commitment to one another, the coaching team, the school, the shared goals, and the community. Groups become teams when the membership is highly cohesive around all of these things**. It is like a vow or pledge to support one another in achieving the team goals but also each person's individual ones. **Without commitment, teams who even wear the same "uniform," if you will, are more likely to fail**.

And, finally, a reminder to all of us is that many **teams have people from disparate backgrounds that help us blend into being the best. Every customer we have—internal and external—is vital to the positive outcomes of the team effort. Your ultimate job is to serve everyone to the best of your ability who comes to you for anything. That is the ultimate "commitment."**[2]

CHAPTER 8

Make the Ultimate Investment

The goal as a company is to have customer service that is not just the best but legendary.

—Sam Walton, American Business Magnate, Founder
of Wal-Mart

After breakfast one morning, the entire group decided to take a stroll by the lake. The plan was to go fishing later in the day when the sun wasn't as hot.

As they walked, they paused from time to time to appreciate the flora and fauna. The untamed and natural beauty of the surroundings brought about a total sense of relaxation.

"There's just something about flowers growing in the wild that's truly captivating," Ray said as he paused to touch the petals. "I believe this is Aster and over there are Bluets."

Liza walked over to take a closer look, "You're right. That's impressive, Ray. You know quite a bit about flowers."

Ray smiled, "Not that much. I did take a few classes in Botanical Science in college and have always been fascinated with flowers."

Liza pointed to a nearby bush, "See those over there. They are Anemone, and the red flower beside it is Columbine."

Ray was impressed, "Those are beautiful. You must share my love of flowers?"

Liza moved to a shady spot under a large tree,

Funny you should ask. I wasn't a big fan of flowers growing up. But, it turned out that during my days as a Customer Research Manager, one of my earliest jobs, the management team wanted to start selling flower seeds in small packets in our stores. My job was to research the most beautiful types of flowers that would grow in our retail locations around the country. To do the job right, with my team, we conducted extensive research visiting several flower farms and even forested areas to validate our findings. All that work made me learn so much about flowers and gave me an appreciation for their uniqueness and beauty like never before.

Ava and Allan joined her under the shady spot.

"I remember those days, mom." Ava said, "You were traveling so much then."

Allan pulled his sunglasses from his pocket, "Oh, yeah. I remember too. Seeing you doing your research in your study late into the night for several months."

Ray adjusted his cap, "That must have been really hard work with a lot of pressure to produce while, at the same time, wanting to be with your family."

Liza nodded,

It was hard, but it was an important part of my job, and I was just getting started in my career. I'm so grateful that my family supported me in my efforts to create a solid work foundation and that they helped me relax and enjoy life too!

I really wanted to find the best products for our customers and also for the company. I think that's an important part of delivering service excellence. You have to *give it 100 percent in every aspect of your work. You need to make an effort to please both internal and external customers. Actually, I think pleasing them is not enough. You have to impress and, better yet, amaze.*

Ray concurred,

Absolutely agree. In fact, my career and those of Glenn and Sergio were built on very hard work and the quest to consistently do exceptional work. Speaking of my pals, I think they are way behind us, let me go check on them.

Ray headed toward Glenn and Sergio who were chatting by a large bush about 20 feet behind them.

Ava turned to Liza, "Mom, wasn't your good work in that role instrumental to your getting that big promotion to Vice President."

Liza smiled,

You have such a good memory. Ultimately, yes with a lot of stops along the way! Our company leadership was quite pleased with the end results. The customers ended up very happy, and product sales skyrocketed. We all worked so hard for that outcome and that includes both of you!

Allan pondered for a bit then said, "Mom, didn't you get that big bonus too as a result of that project and we ended up taking a European vacation?"

Liza laughed,

Yep, you're right. I guess hard work and great customer service really pays off, but it's not just in a monetary way. Providing great customer service is who we ought to be every day—it is so satisfying and motivating and just the right thing to do!

Allan looked at her,

That's exactly why I want to be in a similar career, mom. I'd like *to take on the challenges relating to tough customer service problems and to find amazing solutions.* Rewards would be nice. But, for me it's more about *overcoming challenges and winning the hearts of customers.* I know that sounds idealistic but that's who you raised us to be. I figure to someone out there that will be my customer, *I am the "company" to them,* and I need to hold that responsibility high in my daily interactions.

Liza gave him a hug.

I'm so proud that you allowed me to be your mentor besides the privilege of being your mom. I hope you find a team like so many I have had over the years that shares your passion and skills. I'm very glad you're interested in customer service. There's so much more to do in making positive service improvements in all businesses.

Ava moved a step closer to them,

I'm sure you'll do great, Allan. I've seen your capacity to work hard. Mom, the lessons I learned from you about service—the *importance of hard work, attention to detail, value of research and preparation, the privilege of being on a team and helping it be its best, and the passion to be amazing*—I will also use in my service career.

Liza nodded,

Definitely. It has been my privilege and pleasure to contribute to both your learning and growth. Ava, your desire to make the world a better place is quite admirable. Your work in college has inspired me. I am seriously considering how I can also make an important contribution in government or a nonprofit organization as well. Hopefully, one day. You both inspire me to be better and continue to serve. Regardless of one's title, compensation, and other perks of a job, making our world a better place is why we are here, ultimately, and that responsibility never ends.

The three men approached them.

Ava waved at them and said, "Wow, look at those beautiful butterflies right beside you!"

Three large monarch butterflies fluttered around them as if to welcome them and prod them to explore some more.

"Totally magical," Glenn said, "It's a pity we don't normally take the time to enjoy nature more."

The group proceeded closer to the lake. Then, out of the blue, a huge bass jumped out of the water and made a big splash!

"Wow!" Sergio exclaimed, "Did you see that?"

"Yep" Ray said, "Seems like he's teasing us and asking why aren't you fishing yet?"

Ava laughed, "Why do you think they do that? Jump out of the water?"

Ray maintained his gaze in the vicinity of the jumping bass. "Many reasons. Some are dodging predators, while others are trying to get food or get rid of external parasites. Whatever the reason, it's quite a sight."

Sergio agreed,

Indeed, and it's quite fascinating to suddenly see a splash in this large and quiet expanse of water. There are hundreds, perhaps thousands or even millions of fish in this lake, and one decides to grab our attention! How lucky we are to see that!

The group decided to sit on a large log and enjoy the view of the lake.

"You know," Glenn said,

At times, it pays to grab attention. *In marketing, those that come up with highly creative advertising or special offers get noticed, but they need to follow it up with consistent fantastic service to earn and retain customer loyalty.* I still recall one occasion when I bought some furniture for the house on a weekend after being attracted by their "one day only" sale. The furniture wouldn't fit in my truck, and the salesman offered to deliver it to my house after his shift at no extra cost. I offered to tip him and pay for the gas, but he refused. He even carried the furniture to the precise place in the house where I wanted it and wouldn't take a dime for the extra work after hours. All he said was, "I hope you'll remember me the next time you purchase furniture."

Over the years, I bought more furniture from him and recommended his store and him specifically to several friends. In business, *when you make a splash—by showing true concern and going above and beyond—you'll be remembered and reap the rewards of customer loyalty.* But don't forget, *customers have short memories—your excellent service is quickly replaced by that of another business that equaled or bettered your service level in the customer's mind,* so you and I are constantly taxed with upping our game from interaction to interaction. You will *never have a "permanent customer".*

Liza smiled, "True, in our company, we work hard to assure *every customer interaction is memorable for them—in a positive way,*" she said with a laugh.

Sergio nodded,

Great strategy! I believe it's also important to ensure that the staff are motivated and empowered to consistently deliver such high levels of service. In my hotel chain, staff are empowered to do anything they feel comfortable with to solve problems for customers and maintain their loyalty. We see *problems as opportunities.* They're opportunities to delight customers and enhance their loyalty.

In a hotel, there are many opportunities to do that at modest cost, such as free access to the Executive Lounge or a voucher for dinner all the way up to a complementary stay for their next visit. *Staff should be empowered to do whatever they feel necessary to ensure customers leave satisfied.*

"Couldn't agree more," said Ray.

Many businesses don't understand that highly loyal customers who keep coming back are by far the most profitable customers you can have. As well as avoiding the very high marketing cost of winning new customers, smart companies know that *loyal customers spend more and are less price sensitive because they know that your great service adds value, and they recommend you to their friends and family.*

New customers that you get through personal recommendations are more loyal than those you win through advertising or special offers. In my health and wellness business, we always personally thank the customer who made a referral that ended up in a new customer joining us. And we know that we are always competing with every other business that our customers come in contact with. *Every interaction with even our most loyal customers must be stellar.*

"I see," said Ava.

It seems to me that you're talking about the *difference between long-term and short-term thinking with regard to service.* It is more impactful to do things that may take time to pay off but are much more successful *in the long run.*

Allan was pensive, "It looks like service excellence is largely *about sustainability and longevity* as well."
Sergio smiled,

Speaking of longevity, the three of us may be up there in age, but we're still believers and proponents of customer service. We still have youthful energy and enthusiasm in many ways and continue to care about service.

Glenn chimed in, "Service forever!"

Mastering Customer Service

Insight 8: Investing in Fantastic Service Always Pays in the Long Run

Making the Ultimate Investment

This chapter gives us several reminders about what the "ultimate investment" in ourselves, our career, our job, and our company look like.

Liza reminds us that **every aspect of our work deserves 100 percent of our effort both for internal and external customers**—our goal should always be to impress and amaze. And Allan has learned from his studies and his mentors, including his mom and grandpa, that **challenges and problems allow the opportunity for amazing solutions and winning the hearts of customers**. They have been raised to enjoy the privilege of **being the company** to every customer with whom they interact.

Being "the company" to every customer that you have contact with on any level is the responsibility all of us in customer service have (which is everyone employed anywhere in any position). That attitude will secure customers for your business and enable a great career for you!

Ray reminds us, once again, that **loyal customers spend more and are less price sensitive because they know that your great service adds value, and they recommend you to their friends and family. Every interaction with even your most loyal customers must be stellar.**

Our investment in ourselves, our career, our job, and our company is personal. It's not parroting what you read or learn—it's what you allow to become meaningful to you. It's what matches your values (because you've taken the time to assess what they are and embrace them). It is you—past, present, and future. You are the key to your success and to your customer's service excellence! The "ultimate investment" is in you!

Three Points Within This Chapter Deserve Special Consideration

Why Are Problems the Key to Customer Service?

If the company's customer service is excellent, 78 percent of consumers will do business with them again after a mistake.[1] And when (not if) the company's service is not excellent every time, the "problem" within the lacking service becomes an opportunity to learn, listen, and improve. Fifty percent of customers claim they would switch to a new brand after just one bad experience![2] Your concentration as a service professional is doing your best to serve optimally every time, and when your best was just not good enough, you have a very limited opportunity to regain your customer's loyalty. We have discussed empowerment elsewhere in this book, but a reminder that the best companies that continue to flourish not only provide excellent products but their staff at all levels are empowered to do whatever they feel is necessary to ensure customers leave the interaction satisfied.

Always remember that you are gauging the customer's needs and wants, personality, and values in a few short minutes. And, in return, **many customers judge their relationship with the company based on the warmth of the interaction with the customer service professional with whom they are dealing at that moment.**[3] How you come across with your nonverbals from the very beginning of the interaction (regardless of the medium being used) is critical for exciting the customer and gaining their loyalty.

Nonverbal communication refers to movements, gestures, tone of voice, and other signals that clarify or confuse the meaning of the verbal communication. Nonverbals are either contributors— supporting the intended message—or detractors—inhibiting the receipt of the intended message. In-person detractors to good communication include:

- **Crossed arms**
- **Little or no eye contact**
- **Looking at your watch, phone, and computer**

- **Head shaking**

While you may cross your arms because you are cold or are more introverted and so don't make eye contact easily or shake your head to connote that you hear what is being said—not necessarily agree, your customer may see someone who is not engaged in the interaction. **Realizing your nonverbals that may unintentionally detract from positive engagement with your customer is vital as you may not get a second chance at first impressions.**

Contributors to enhance the interaction and better assure that the intended message is received include:

- **Relaxed posture**
- **Good eye contact**
- **Look of concern as appropriate**
- **Smiling**
- **Nodding with acknowledgment**

Granted any of these can be misread as well. Relaxed posture can appear that you are not taking the situation seriously. Good eye contact doesn't mean a stare-down. Smiling continuously can appear patronizing, and the nodding head needs to be clarified that "I hear what you are saying—I don't necessarily agree." So, using nonverbals to your advantage and that of the customer takes practice, awareness of the current situation, and the willingness to modify your approach on the spur of the moment.

But one of the **most important nonverbals that is applicable to any medium where information is being exchanged is voice tone.** In the written word, "great" has to mean "wonderful." It can be misread to be sarcastic and completely change your intended message so support "great" with other wording that reinforces your communication thrust.

And if you are speaking with someone and lack the in-person contact that allows the customer to read the aforementioned nonverbals to assess the intended message, **assure that your voice is always calm, pitched at a rate and volume that is comfortable for the listener but not demeaning.**

Finally listen more than you speak. Good listening includes:

- **Paraphrasing or speaking back as appropriate to confirm what the customer is saying so that they know you heard and understood**
- **Asking appropriate questions to clarify**
- **Balancing talking and listening**
- **Summarizing at the end of the other person's statement what the crux of the issue is and next steps/responsible parties/timeline**

It takes a wide variety of skills to be an effective customer service professional and at the top is the ability to communicate effectively. It takes awareness, learning, practice, and flexibility, but the rewards are phenomenal for all involved.[4]

What Is the Impact of Having Long-Term Versus Short-Term Thinking When It Comes to Customer Service?

While most of us are looking for the **immediate and positive response to an issue presented to us, looking at the long term (having a loyal customer for a lifetime) is the ultimate goal**. One interaction at a time. If your focus is strictly on getting this customer out the door, your short-term thinking will sink the ship. You should **always be thinking about sustainability and longevity of every relationship opportunity.**

Ninety-three percent of customers are likely to make repeat purchases with companies that offer excellent customer service.[1] That should and must be your long-term goal based on the short-term moments you have with each customer. Your job isn't to just assure the customer is satisfied with this interaction but that you **thoughtfully and perhaps retrospectively reflect on how to head off an issue you sense is brewing**. Twenty-two percent of repeat calls involve downstream issues related to the problem that prompted the original call even if that problem itself was adequately addressed the first time around.[5]

A great example of this concept is that many calls back to a business have to do with a product purchased whose instructions may be confusing. Developing quick/simple tutorials on how to use the product saves everyone time, and the customer feels enabled to truly complete their purchase to their satisfaction.

Fifty-seven percent of inbound calls come from customers who went to the company's website first but found it difficult to navigate.[5] Too many businesses don't take the time to keep their website up-to-date and expend little effort troubleshooting it to make sure it is easily used by even the least experienced customer. **Make it easy to do business with your company by assuring that your primary "face"—your website—is clear, current, easy to use, and contains answers to the primary issues your customer service professionals find themselves answering every day.**

Your daily mission must be focusing on reducing customer effort, which is focused on the long term and accomplished with every short-term interaction.

What Are the Global Behaviors I Should Be Displaying to Assure I Am Providing the Best Customer Service?

Seventy percent of the customer's journey is based on how the customer feels they are being treated, and 90 percent of consumers worldwide consider issue resolution as their most crucial customer service concern.[1] We also know that great customer experience requires cross-functional collaboration and fewer silos.[2]

So what are the winning behaviors for customer service professionals to consistently provide in order to gather, retain, and enjoy customer loyalty?

- **Be a willing and participating member of numerous teams** within your company to better assure that customers get the best "you" through the knowledge and experience of you and your teammates.
- **Assure enough but not too much interaction with the customer.** Gauge the needed amount of time with the customer based on the issue at hand, the tone of the customer, the level of empowerment you hold and so on. Push away the temptation

to think about all of the other "to do's" you have and solve the issue at hand or, at the least, move it to the next reasonable level of resolution which will satisfy the customer. Overwhelming the customer with too complex a process to send a simple message or requiring them to spend extra effort navigating a difficult system will likely be viewed as "too much" by the customer. A loss you may not be able to afford.

- **Reduce the urge to save money by becoming too automated with customers doing most of the work.**[5]
- **Pay attention to details.**
- **Be prepared before returning a customer call**. Know their issues, their likely preferences, the best way to approach, and satisfy their needs and wants. Do your research! If you don't have those answers, someone on your team does—the benefit of a team!
- **Make a "splash" with every interaction by showing true concern and going above and beyond**. That will make you a memorable customer service professional in a good way! You never have a "permanent" customer, so "splashing" with every interaction is imperative for your longevity and personal satisfaction and that of those around you let alone producing happy customers.
- Someone must **be in control of the satisfactory resolution** to any issue and that is the customer service professional's job.
- **Assess, develop, practice, and constantly improve your communication style** so that it comfortably suits you and every person with whom you come in contact. Be flexible.
- **Enjoy what you do—you are worth a good day every day!**

CHAPTER 9

Motivate and Empower

The best executive is the one who has sense enough to pick good men to do what he wants done and self-restraint to keep from meddling with them while they do it.

—Theodore Roosevelt, 26th U.S. President

Several uneventful days followed. Like clockwork, the group spent their days having coffee and cereal in the morning. They then proceeded with their daily stroll by the lake.

Late mornings were spent either reading books, speaking with family, or playing cards.

Lunch largely consisted of soup and sandwiches.

After a little nap, the group would proceed to their favorite fishing spot.

So far, the catch had always been impressive. They were able to snag a wide array of fish of various sizes. Ray had the honor of being the top fisherman consistently bagging more than five catches per outing.

The trip rekindled the men's friendship. Sergio and Ray became very close with Glenn's family. Liza called them lifetime honorary members of their clan.

Ava and Allan helped the men organize the photographs they took from their cellphones and cameras. They built a large catalog of photos, some utterly hilarious. Mementos of the great summer fun they had together.

There were several meaningful conversations about their life journeys as well as plans for future get-togethers.

Ava and Allan grew very close to the men and became valued members of their team. The three retired men referred to both of them as their most valued persons. Because Ava so enjoyed cooking, she volunteered to take the lead role in ensuring everyone had good meals, stayed hydrated, and that the older men consistently took their medications. Allan made sure they had the fishing supplies, travel bags, and emergency kits with them. At some point, Ray jokingly said, "We'd probably end up dead if Ava and Allan weren't around."

During the evenings, they enjoyed a lot more flexibility, especially during dinner time. Some nights were spent having barbecues by the campfire. Others having meals in the dining room. And some were simply spent having a "light" snack and beer or wine on the porch. The "light" snack consisted of a handful of carrots and celery and loads of ham, cheese, salami, and crackers. Sergio likes to call those meals the "healthy option," and they laughed quite a bit about it.

Tonight was a "healthy option" night. And, as they sat by the porch, heavy rain started to fall, followed by thunder and lightning.

Liza walked from the kitchen to the porch to join them. She looked at the weather app on her phone and said, "Looks like there's a storm coming."

Glenn was concerned, "How bad is it supposed to get?"

Liza looked bothered, "A nasty one that will likely run all through the night. Perhaps until morning."

Glenn tried to calm her, "Well, at least we're secured in this fortress of a home."

Liza smiled weakly, "Mostly, yes. Although there were years where storms broke some of the glass windows and caused some flooding. Hopefully, it's not going to be one of those. I'll keep tracking the storm and alert everyone."

She turned to Ava and Allan, "Guys, let's get the emergency lamps and other supplies ready."

The three of them headed hurriedly inside the house.

"We'll stay out here for a bit then follow you in," Glenn said.

The group were discussing playing cards that evening when they saw a pick-up truck heading toward the cabin.

Driven by instinct, Glenn stood up and pulled out his gun from the bag, "We can never be too sure. Who would come to this isolated place during a storm and at night?"

He turned to Liza and yelled toward the kitchen, "Liza are you expecting someone? A car just pulled up the driveway."

Liza responded, "No, I'm not expecting anyone. Who would drive out in a major storm?"

She walked toward the porch to join the men.

They all looked at the vehicle as it slowed down. The unexpected visit bothered them all.

The truck stopped, and a man stepped out soaking wet in the rain, "Liza? It's Dave!"

Liza could hardly see him or hear his voice in the pouring rain.

The man yelled loudly, "It's Dave from Johnson Maintenance."

Liza was surprised, "Oh, hi Dave! What are you doing here in the storm?"

She turned to the men, "It's Dave. His company is the contractor that handles the maintenance of the houses in this area."

Liza walked toward Dave, "Dave come in. You're all wet. What brought you here tonight?"

"Sorry to disturb you, Liza" Dave said apologetically,

I tried to call but couldn't get through. The phone signal is all messed up. There's a major storm coming. I wanted to make sure you're aware. They didn't call for an evacuation or anything like that yet, but the newscaster on the radio just said that it might be a possibility. I wanted to board up some of your glass windows … the ones that had major damage last time.

Liza was touched, "Oh, thank you so much, Dave. You didn't have to come over for this. Its raining so hard. You live like 20 miles away."

Dave started getting his equipment from the truck,

Oh, don't worry about it. When I heard about the storm, the first thing that came to mind was your large glass windows. It caused a huge mess during the last big storm. Let me board them up real quick, and I'll be out of your way. Wanted to make sure you're safe and the property somewhat protected.

"Thank you so much, Dave." Liza said earnestly.

Oh, I almost forgot." Dave said, "I brought you a spare generator on the truck and lots of fuel. I also brought a radio and a box of canned food and bottled water. I'll set up the radio so that you can reach me anytime.

Glenn approached Dave, "Dave, we really appreciate the help. Anything we can do to help?"

Dave shook his head, "Nope, I got this. Just say safe and dry. I'll get this done and be out of your way in a jiffy. There are a couple of other nearby houses I wanted to check out as well."

Glenn was impressed by Dave's kindness and efficiency, "We very much appreciate this, Dave. You didn't have to go out of your way to do this."

Dave shook his head and said sincerely, "But, I do. I treat all my clients like family and want to make sure they are safe and the property protected during times like this. I'll get started now. This won't take too long."

Dave boarded up the glass windows in about 30 minutes.

The men helped Dave move the generator, radio, and food provisions into the house.

The group expressed their gratitude.

"Dave, you are such a kind soul," Glenn said, "Thank you so much for looking after us."

"You're most welcome" Dave said, "Oops, I almost forgot."

He ran back to the truck and brought back a small box. "Compliments from my wife, Jill. She loves baking, and when she heard that you have guests over, Liza, she made you a chocolate cake."

Liza took the box, "Dave, you and your wife are unbelievable. Thank you so much."

Dave smiled, "No problem. The radio is now set up and so is the generator. Call me if you need anything."

Liza looked at Dave gratefully, "We will. Drive safely, Dave. You're welcome to stay a bit if you'd like to wait for the rain to subside."

As Dave walked toward his truck he said,

Thanks, I have to head out to help a couple of other houses. There isn't anyone living in them at the moment and I want to make sure they are as secure from damage as possible. Have a good evening all and stay safe! Tune in the radio station in case they issue an evacuation order.

In a flash, Dave and his truck disappeared out of sight.

"Well, what do you know," Sergio said, "It was just as if an angel stepped in to protect us and brought us gifts to boot."

Glenn placed his gun back in the bag. "He was indeed quite like an angel, and I really didn't need this gun after all."

Sergio took a peek at the boxed cake and said jokingly, "More healthy options!"

Everyone laughed.

The group decided to move to the family room to play cards.

Allan continued the conversation about Dave,

Businesspersons like Dave are unusual these days. In my business classes, we're taught to carefully watch the bottom line and think about profitability. Dave's actions were in direct contrast to that concept. Yet, in my view, the way he runs his business is superior.

"It's unusual in large organizations, Allan, because it is viewed as unnecessary expense" said Ray.

And even in small businesses that have direct contact with their customers, it is a challenge. If you think about it, the great service we have received this holiday has all come from small businesses—the diner on the way, the garage, the B&B, and now Dave. The challenge for many corporations is to replicate that level of service across their much larger organizations where many, often most staff, don't have direct contact with customers.

Ava agreed, "In service careers, a mindset and attitude like Dave's can transform organizations. It would enhance operational performance and lead to impactful results. Dave would be an inspiration in any workplace."

Sergio thought for a minute and said,

One thing that was impressive about Dave was the *confidence he exuded*. He was determined to beat the storm and make it here. He was confident that he could board up the glass windows quickly. He was confident that the radio and generator might be needed and would work if called on. He was confident that he would be able to help the other homes. He knew what he wanted to do and had the *courage and willpower to make it happen*. With the right kind of confidence, amazing things can happen in one's life and career.

Glenn took a sip of beer and said,

In my military career, I have observed that those who had the right service attitude and the *right dose of confidence* ended up quite successful. Moreover, if they possess the *leadership ability to build confidence in others and empower them* to do the right thing, then the level of accomplishment doubles. In an organization, this means that instead of one person delivering results, it would be one big group of people accomplishing amazing results.

Sergio shuffled the deck of cards then spoke,

I would describe men like Dave as *straightforward—genuine and authentic*. They run their business based on who they really are. Individuals and companies that do that truly make their mark with every interaction. One of the benefits Dave has is that he is his own boss and can, therefore, empower himself to do whatever he feels needs to be done. Unfortunately, that just isn't the way it works in most businesses. Sometimes lines of communication get snarled, and efficiency and effectiveness suffer.

Glenn pondered and said,

I agree with you, Sergio. Regardless of how much someone wants to be empowered, if leadership doesn't recognize that or support it, the effort will get lost, and the employee will likely move on to another organization that embraces true but clear empowerment.

In my military career, I've known numerous people who consistently upheld the *highest standards of integrity*. They didn't play politics but endeavored to do what was right and what they thought was best with every interaction. A good lesson for us all! My brother says he would be ashamed if he ever returned a car to a customer that wasn't in perfect condition. That includes an immaculate valet, however dirty the vehicle was when it arrived. He says it *never pays to cut corners so that you can advertise the cheapest price.*

Ava agreed, "I just read a quote from Douglas Adams a few days back that said—to give real service you must add something which cannot be bought or measured by money, and that is *sincerity and integrity.*"
Liza smiled,

That's a nice one. One of my favorite customer service quotes was from Benjamin Franklin—it takes many good deeds to build a good reputation, and only one bad one to lose it. Integrity is doing the right thing, especially when no one is watching.

Ray filled a small plate with an assortment of meat and cheese,

I wish more people embraced the insight from those quotes. In the medical industry, there have been some cases of practitioners who sold their soul to commercialize a product or service. They prioritized money over their commitment to health and wellness. Fortunately, at the end of the day, those lost souls got caught and paid the price. *False claims and pretenses always have an expiration date.*

Sergio joined him but picked the carrots and celery instead,

I read a study some time ago that *over 90 percent of global consumers reward brands they see as authentic, that consistently live their values.* In my hotel chain, we make sure that we hire the kind of people that embrace our service values. Our policy is to *recruit for attitude and train for skills.* To consistently deliver a great experience to customers, our hotels need to be staffed by people who naturally want to help others.

Allan agreed,

In one of the marketing classes I took, we talked about exceptional customer service where a company provides unconditional commitment to top quality service regardless of the situation. In class, we discussed the case of Trader Joe's. A woman wanted to get a low-sodium meal to her dad who was snowed in during the holidays. No grocery store would deliver. The Trader Joe's team decided to push their standard practice and delivered the meal to the gentleman in under 30 minutes—free of charge. In this case, the operational empowerment given to the customer service staff by the company allowed them to provide the level of service that aligned well with the company's brand. That family will spread positive comments about Trader Joe's more than any formal PR firm ever could!

Glenn agreed, "*When companies embrace a truly caring and empowering culture and set up conditions where customers are prioritized, real magic happens.*"

Mastering Customer Service

Insight 9: Recruit, Motivate, and Empower the Right People

Recruiting

In the first chapter of this book, we said that customer service is fundamentally about helping people, so delivering great customer service starts with employing the right people. **Frontline customer service staff especially must be outward-looking people who derive great pleasure from helping others.** This is much more important than skills and experience. An inward-looking self-centered person will never deliver great service, regardless of how efficient and experienced they are.

At a conference one of the authors attended, Professor James Heskett from Harvard Business School explained how a major U.S. company recruited frontline customer service staff. They assembled the applicants in a room, sitting around a table like a discussion group. The facilitator asked each person in the group to tell everybody about their most distressing memory. The facilitator, and colleagues behind the one-way mirror, had no interest in the experiences the applicants described. Instead, when each person was relating their story, the panel was studying the reactions of the other applicants. Those who remained impassive, probably concentrating on thinking up their own dramatic story, clearly did not have the right attitude. By contrast, those who showed empathy, perhaps getting upset as the tragic story unfolded, were the ones selected for employment. Skill and experience were not discussed with the applicants. As Professor Heskett said, "**recruit for attitude, train for skills.**"[1] For frontline customer service roles, if you've recruited the kind of people who want to help others, it is relatively straight forward to train them to have the relevant skills for the job.

Motivating

Recruiting the right people makes motivating much easier. They're intrinsically motivated to help others. Having said that, it is good to have bonuses for the right behaviors and outcomes, but if you've recruited frontline customer service employees with the right attitudes the main purpose of bonuses is to reward rather than motivate, but they will still serve to reinforce the behaviors that come naturally to those who want to help others. To work well, bonuses should be linked as closely as possible to the desired outcomes, they should be transparent, and they should be timely. If staff have to wait a year for a bonus, the scheme will make little, if any difference to their day-to-day behavior at work. Before its acquisition by Bank of America,[2] credit card provider MBNA bonused its call center staff on customer satisfaction, which the company measured daily. Every day that the customer satisfaction score was above target, staff qualified for bonus. The next day as they arrived at work, employees could see the previous day's satisfaction score prominently displayed, so they knew straight away if they had exceeded target and had earned a bonus, and if they hadn't hit the target, they had another chance to earn it today. Every day that they arrived at work was another opportunity to earn a bonus if they gave customers great service. The daily bonuses that the call handlers had earned were all added to their salary at the end of each month, so they didn't have long to wait for it either.[1]

As we said earlier, the bonus is primarily designed to reward rather than to motivate. If you have recruited the right kind of people that want to give great service to help others, it will be their ability to do the right thing for customers that will be their main motivation—and for that to happen they need to be empowered to do it.

Empowering

Frontline customer service staff like to be trusted. The thing they hate the most at work is if they are constrained from doing what they know needs to happen to satisfy the customer because systems or procedures get in the way or simply because they are not empowered to do it. Empowerment does not mean "carte blanche." There do need to be boundaries on what they can do, but within limits, they have to be empowered to use their judgment on a customer-by-customer basis to do whatever they think is necessary to make the customer satisfied. What they are empowered to do and what limits are set will depend on the strategy of the business. For example, they may or may not have a budget to reduce the customer's bill if service fell short or to reward some customers with extra benefits.

Fairfield Inns has a long history of empowering staff to do whatever they feel is necessary to make guests satisfied. Formed in 1987 as an "economy-limited service" hotel chain, its original CEO, Mel Warriner defined the mission as having the friendliest employees and cleanest rooms anywhere for a price of no more than $39.95 per night. Its primary target market at that time was "road warriors," frequent business travelers who would become loyal customers, bringing the company the 3R benefits of retention, repeat business, and referrals. Recruitment of amazing staff was the first challenge in achieving this ambitious objective. Key to delivering the promise were the housekeepers, but they had to be far more than just cleaners. As well as being passionate about cleanliness, they also had to be very friendly and keen to help their guests and be happy to have their performance constantly monitored. This was done by guests rating their stay, including cleanliness and staff friendliness on departure. Warriner later said that only 1 in 24 applicants fitted his job specification, but those who did were rewarded with higher wages than paid by competitors in the budget hotel industry, which also reduced turnover.[3]

Since the 3Rs of customer loyalty were such an important part of the company's business plan, he needed housekeepers to be prominent members of staff playing a key part in guest relations. Warriner needed them to get to know frequent visitors, especially those "road warriors" covering a regional business territory. To help them, they were given a "guest amenities budget," enabling them to spend modest amounts of money to leave little treats in the rooms of loyal customers. To do this, of course, they had to get to know guests well enough to know what kind of treats would be appreciated by them.

As a consequence of these enlightened initiatives, Fairfield Inns reduced costs through lower staff turnover and lower management costs as frontline staff mostly managed themselves. **This level of trust and empowerment made them more motivated and gave them great job satisfaction, which resulted in them delivering better service to customers. The great service increased guest satisfaction and**

loyalty, and the 3Rs resulted in higher customer lifetime value.
In recent times, the customer lifetime value of loyal hotel guests has
been measured as $57,000[4] and as long ago as the 1980s, Carl Sewell
famously estimated the lifetime value of a loyal customer at his Cadillac
dealership to be £332,000.[5]

Harvard has named this process **the human resources value cycle,**[3]
but to achieve the business benefits of higher customer satisfaction,
loyalty, and profit, **the three crucial stages of human resource
management that we have identified—recruitment, motivation, and
empowerment—need to be executed to world class standards.**

CHAPTER 10

Make Every Interaction Positive

Do a little bit of good where you are; it's those little bits of good put together that overwhelm the world.

—Desmond Tutu, South African Bishop

The storm passed by midmorning the next day. Thankfully, no evacuation plans were issued, but the group had been prepared should leaving quickly be required.

Liza radioed Dave and informed him that the wooden planks he installed protected the glass windows. There was no damage at the house other than several trees that fell. Dave promised he'd take care of those in the next couple of days. Liza thanked him again and offered to return the supplies he kindly and thoughtfully left for them, but Dave insisted she keep the radio and generator for the time being—just in case.

Around lunchtime the group converged in the kitchen.

Ray shared with everyone some of the best photos of the trip. Ava and Allan offered to put together a short video commemorating their time together.

"I had a blast," Sergio said, "It was nice to see my buddies after all these years and reminisce on the good old days. I enjoyed staying in this beautiful home and hanging out with this lovely family. I really don't want to leave."

Liza smiled,

I'm so glad you like it here. We really enjoyed having you with us. The kids and I had a lot of fun and we learned so much from you. I especially am reminded that even the best job, company, career can run its course, and when you feel that happening, start planning for the next stage in your life. That has given me so much peace, and I'm excited to see where the next 20 years will take me. I'll want to pick all of your brains on that as the plan begins to solidify.

And the timing was perfect for having you all here. You're always welcome anytime. Perhaps another visit next summer?

Ray sipped on his iced tea, "That would be wonderful! I think the fish in the lake won't be too happy to hear that I'll be heading back next year."

Everyone laughed.

Sergio suggested, "Well, we could give the fish a break and take a European trip together instead!"

Glenn was excited, "That would be a lot of fun! We'd need to bring our most valued persons with us though. Not sure what would happen to us without them."

Ava couldn't hide her enthusiasm, "I'd love to go. Especially if grandpa is paying."

Glenn smiled, "Consider it done. I'm paying for Liza, Allan, and Ava for sure. I'm sure these gentlemen would take offense if I paid for theirs."

Ray and Sergio shook their heads and said in unison, "No we won't."

Glenn laughed, "Ok, no problem. I'm paying for everybody. I think we'll have a great time."

Ray had an idea, "How about you pay for the airfare, Glenn? I pay for all the lodging, and Sergio pays for the meals. Is that okay with you, Sergio?"

Sergio smiled, "Most definitely. Happy to do so. It would be a lot of fun!"

Liza was delighted,

Thank you so much, guys, but I'm covering my own expenses. I've worked so very hard to be able to do that and am proud that I can! You go right ahead and cover the kids' expenses though!

Ray was quick to respond.

Thank you so much to all of you. You've made our vacation a truly amazing experience. Can't wait for the European adventure. Let's start planning it on the way home! And thank you for making Sergio and me honorary family members.

Everyone laughed.

After lunch, the group headed to their rooms for their customary afternoon relaxation.

They regrouped by the poolside later in the evening.

Allan and Ava were clearing some of the storm's debris in the pool when the men arrived. The pool was filled with floating leaves and branches.

The men helped them out, and the pool was back in shape in no time.

They sat in the pool chairs and surveyed some of the damage brought about by the storm.

Glenn pointed toward the direction of the tall trees, "Looks like quite a number of trees fell. Dave will be busy."

Ava peered at the night sky and exclaimed, "Look! A shooting star!"

The men quickly huddled beside her to take a look. Allan joined them. The meteor's streaking bright light stayed visible in the horizon for several seconds for all to see.

Ray was elated, "What a grand way to cap our time together."

He grabbed a beer and said, "Cheers!"

The others reciprocated enthusiastically.

Sergio said,

Well Ava and Allan, we've talked a lot about life in general and ours specifically. I hope you enjoyed the trip and learned something about service careers from us as well. Where do you stand on the career direction you are leaning toward?

Ava nodded,

I believe I've made my decision. Over the past few days, I have been fascinated by your collective commitment to serve others. Ray, as a doctor you saved many lives and promoted health and wellness around the world. Sergio, you educated thousands of students and readers through your classrooms, books, and research. You spread valuable knowledge around the world. Grandpa, your work contributed to the safety and security of our country and led to peace in many corners of the world. I am inspired by your chosen field and the many contributions you have made to our country's safety. I've decided to follow a similar path to the one you took and embark on a service career as a diplomat. I've been offered an entry level position at the U.S. Embassy in Turkey and am excited to begin my customer service career there.

Glenn looked at her proudly, "I'm sure you'll love it and do an amazing job! I couldn't be happier for you."

The men concurred.

"As for me" Allan said,

I'm also convinced that a career with a service angle would be right for me. I am positive I would love to work as a Customer Service Manager and take on a path similar to mom's. I learned a lot from you all this summer and from mom my whole life. You guys gave me a truly valuable graduation present in the form of service insights. Thank you so much.

Glenn gave Allan a hug, "You're welcome, Allan. Glad we could be of some help. You made a great choice. That role will suit you very well. And what a role model in your mom!"

"Good luck to both of you!" Ray and Sergio said in unison.

"Hopefully, some of the insights we offered will guide you along the way." Glenn said.

Ava sat on the lounge chair,

I'm sure they will. Probably more than you could imagine. I took a mental note of all of them and then captured them on my laptop to refer to over and over. My boyfriend, Jake, is starting a digital marketing company. I've been sharing with him some of the things I learned from you all about service excellence in companies, and he's already talking about how very helpful they are. He's started using some of them already!

Sergio sat beside her,

That's great. There's one more lesson I'd like to share with both of you. Remember the shooting star we just saw? *When it comes to service excellence, don't just be a shooting star.* You need to deliver consistently good effort over the long term. Your *good work should be impactful, sustainable, and reliable.* This approach works for careers as well as companies. In careers, your superiors should be able to count on you to *perform well at all times and not just on certain occasions like when someone is watching.*

In companies, great service should not just happen sometimes but all of the time. One bad service experience can ruin a reputation. I'm sure you've searched online at some point to find restaurants. Did you ever read through some of the reviews and notice their overall star rating? I've seen establishments getting mostly four or five stars as well as a couple of one- or two-star ratings. Despite how many 4s and 5s we see, we start doubting the quality of the product or service when we see any 1s or 2s. Companies nowadays, especially at the onset of the digital revolution and prevalence of social media, really must strive to consistently deliver top quality service. That means *hiring the right people and assuring that your customer service mantra of excellence is embedded in the culture.*

Glenn opened a bottled water and took a sip,

In all companies and jobs including the military, there will always be a few errors and the opportunity to learn and grow from mistakes, but excellent performance over time is the key to *getting critical jobs done right the first time;* let alone getting promotions. Sometimes our nation's safety depended on exactly that.

Ray joined Glenn,

I could say the same about the medical profession. Nowadays, you see star ratings for doctors as well. Potential patients can see feedback from other patients on the kind of service the doctor has provided. Even one bad review can destroy a practice. In some ways, *reviews are good since they provide transparency and push service providers to elevate their game.*

Doctors today have to make a conscious effort to deliver high-quality and caring service with every interaction and must pay attention to what patients are saying. And never forget that while the doctor may lead the team, they are only one member, and *everyone on the team affects the quality of patient outcomes. Remember that to the customer whomever they are dealing with at that moment is "the company."* Reviews reflect that—we are judged as a department and as a company and not just as an individual with every single interaction. So *always make sure that your whole team has the same philosophy and practice of service excellence as you do.* Even though you may not be able to "force" someone to change their approach for the better, you can always try to *influence them with your consistent positive attitude toward service excellence.*

Sergio moved toward the pool and picked up a piece of debris,

To some extent, the academic world is similar to the military. Tenured positions and promotions are carefully decided, and a consistent track record of top quality work is a defining criteria.

While we work independently within our academic setting, one bad experience with a professor anywhere in the institution will be posted on social media, and we are all held accountable to some extent for the service error.

Ava listened to the men intently.

Thank you all for the additional insights on service excellence. I'll certainly make it a point to *always deliver my very best over the long term with every interaction and not just on average.* I will also remember that *anyone who comes to me for anything, whether internal or external, is my customer and deserves my best efforts.* I plan to keep learning and growing so that I can better serve my organization and others and myself! I also realize that it won't be easy to maintain these goals when I get into the real world where so many elements are impacting my ability to deliver excellence at every turn. I plan to watch for opportunities to work through barriers and help others succeed too.

Allan joined her. "One insight I gained is the importance of not just one single act of service excellence but the multitude of them. There has to be *consistency and continuity. Service excellence has to be a habit.*"

Ray smiled, "By the way, just so you'll both know. Based on the quality of work you did for us in the past few weeks, we're giving you both five stars."

Ava laughed, "Thank you. I think I'll head to bed early. It's a long trip tomorrow. But, before I sleep I'll be thinking long and hard about my future and the possibilities it holds."

Allan stood up, "As our mentors and career coaches this summer, we're giving you all five stars as well. Better yet—Career Coaches of the Year. I'll get a plaque made for each of you and Ava, and I will sign it."

Liza overhead the conversation as she joined the group, "Hey, I'll sign it too!"

Mastering Customer Service

Insight 10: *Make Every Interaction a Positive One*

Making Every Interaction Positive

We're reminded throughout this chapter that service excellence is never a one-time thing—like when you think about it, or if you're having a good day, or if you particularly enjoy that customer. If you fall victim to any of those scenarios, you are never going to find success in any position you hold because you are missing the **basic tenet of why any of us work: to do our best regardless of the current assignment**. Our personal dignity deserves that.

Sergio tells us that when it comes to service excellence, we can't just be a **shooting star**. Without consistent delivery of our best effort, your occasional excellence will be seen as a behavior that your customers, co-workers, and the company cannot count on, so your stabs at providing excellent service will be discounted very quickly. You'll get no credit for those efforts and may even damage your reputation further because your inconsistency will be very apparent.

Ray suggests that in our new world of transparency and associated social media ratings, we are all pushed to **elevate our game with every interaction**. That is true regardless of your job, your level of education and experience, your title, whether you wear a business suit or a uniform. We are all "the company" when interacting with the customer, and our less-than-stellar performance will too likely appear on a social media site with potential exaggeration regarding the event. And many others will read, and some will believe the post deciding that you aren't a company with whom they want to do business.

Thus is the privilege of those doing the writing on social media. They can and do **express their displeasure more often than their positive experiences**. And you may be the recipient of their bad day (or yours). Perhaps your service was OK but not good or great. OK service was the last straw that day and stuck with them as they went home—you ended up being their point of focus for a bad review.

It is said that each Facebook profile has an average of 338 friends, so one negative review can quickly reach thousands of people![1] Your business and you cannot afford very many of those events. If you are going to be highlighted in social media, make it for your excellent service and not an "OK" one (or a truly bad one) that loses you customers.

Three Points Within This Chapter Deserve Special Consideration

How Do We Assure Consistency of Excellence When It Comes to Customer Service?

Several times in this book, we have talked about the importance of knowing who you are; what values you embrace that feel right to you; how you play those out every day; what impact your personality, knowledge, attitude, and experience have on guiding your day-to-day behaviors. But the **bottom line is: Are you a person of integrity?**

There are many definitions of **integrity** but perhaps the most practical and meaningful is:

Doing the right thing through your words, actions, and beliefs, particularly when no one is watching. That means being trustworthy and reliable as you practice and encourage open, honest, and respectful communication.[2]

People with integrity as one of their core values consistently earn trust because they are, first and foremost, trustworthy. See if these **characteristics of being trustworthy** "feel" like you:

- **Consistently dependable and reliable**
- **Willingly responsible**
- **Consistently truthful and honest (but not brutally so)**
- **Consistently honorable**

These characteristics (also known as values) drive your attitude through thick and thin, good and bad. So how do these values and associated behaviors impact service excellence? Ninety-six percent of consumers consider customer service to be a crucial factor when deciding whether to remain loyal to a particular brand.[1] While you cannot force others to behave as you do, you can and will definitely **influence them with your consistent positive attitude toward service excellence**.

Whatever your job function is at any given moment, say to yourself "I will do it right the first time" because you may not be given the opportunity to do it over with that customer. You deserve the benefit of your own efficiency and effectiveness and so do your customers!

Decide to form the habit of service excellence assuring that your work is always impactful, sustainable, and reliable. Your company hires you because they expect to be able to count on you to perform well at all times and not just on certain occasions like when someone is watching. You want to be the "right person" that they hired as evidenced by your consistent pursuit of excellence. **Don't ever allow "OK" or "average" to be your standard as you have automatically lowered your own worth**. Always deliver your very best over the long term with every interaction to whomever comes to you for anything—internal or external customers are all vital to not just the business and its success but also to your positive outcomes.

How Do You Know If You Are Hiring the "Right People"?

If you are a hiring agent in your company, you are **seeking the following in those you are bringing onto the team to assure they are the epitome of customer service excellence:**

- People who have a track record of **"being" the right people**.
- They have examples and commensurate behaviors that reflect how they **increase loyalty and satisfaction** with their customers.
- They work to **understand their customers** to better assure they can deliver their needs and wants.
- They **deliver high-quality support, which includes very short turnaround time** on responses promised.
- They **assess their performance and acknowledge and fix their mistakes**.
- They **listen**.

- They **empathize.**
- They are **innovative.**[1]

They serve as a **willing role model without arrogance or titled authority,** realizing that the entire team/workforce must all be on the same page to assure that service excellence is truly embedded in the culture and is the day-to-day mantra.

And, perhaps most importantly, **they make the promises they can keep and keep the promises they make.**[3]

Of course, as the hiring agent, you are looking for demographics as they fit the open position like education, required license(s), and appropriate experience, but remember that those elements are only the very basics to even get their foot in the interview door. Ultimately, with the basics being met, you should **hire based on attitude and proof of being onboard with and acting as a living example of customer service excellence.**

How Do I Help My Company Put Emphasis on Doing the Job Right the First Time?

If you are looking for a new job or career, assess not only whether the job for which you are applying fits your wants and needs as well as your credentials and monetary expectations but, more importantly, does its culture match your values? If the latter answer is "I'm not sure" or "no," look elsewhere because you will not be happy with that employer, and they are likely to not appreciate you to the extent that you deserve.

Part of the cultural elements you are assessing include efficiency and effectiveness. **Efficiency is defined as:**

The ability to achieve an end goal with little-to-no wasted effort or energy. Being efficient means you can achieve your results by using the resources you have in the best way possible. Put simply, something is efficient if nothing is wasted, and all processes are optimized.

And effectiveness means:

The degree to which a desired result is successful.

If we assume that all companies who wish to be successful, profitable, remain in business have, as one of their goals, high customer satisfaction, then "effectiveness" to them is exactly that—a "desired result." **Every interaction with the customer should strive to "do it right the first time." And that is accomplished with efficiency of effort.**

So how can you **assist your company in finding efficiency and effectiveness? Apply these four key factors**[4]:

1. **Resources: Assess the budget and define goals accordingly.** Share the goals throughout the organization so that everyone is on the same page and then hire the right people to get the jobs done efficiently and effectively.
2. **Time:** Be realistic on what your people and machines can do within given timeframes. **Establish production timelines** accordingly. Hire the right people to get those jobs done efficiently and effectively.
3. **Quality:** Establish **challenging and yet reachable quality standards**, educate staff on those standards, and hold them accountable at all levels.
4. **Completeness**: Constantly review how you are doing in meeting set timelines but also with customer satisfaction. **The job is not complete if your efficiency and effectiveness standards are not met.**

Explore with the hiring agent how they maximize efficiency within the workplace. Do they assess delays and how do they respond, do they survey customer satisfaction and listen to the input, are they continuously quality improvement-minded? Do they link efficiency and effectiveness with their training and reward systems? Do they know and focus on critical elements of every job assuring they are appropriately supported for ultimate efficiency and effectiveness?

These are the keys to customer satisfaction—internal and external—and as a potential employee, you can assess them. **As an existing employee, you can aid in their accomplishment expanding your usefulness to the team and for yourself. A win-win!**

CHAPTER 11

Leverage Communication

Seek first to understand, then to be understood.
—Stephen Covey, American educator, author, and businessman

Later that evening, Allan and Ava knocked on Glenn's door. He welcomed them into his room. Glenn was reading in bed, and Ava sat on the end of the bed while Allan sat in a nearby chair.

"Grandpa," Ava said. "Allan and I have been talking a lot over the past couple of weeks—frankly, more than we have in years. We blamed that on busy school schedules and internships, but, in reality, we prioritized other things above family."

"Yes," Allan added.

We fell into the routine that a text message here and there and maybe even an occasional phone call was all of the catching up we needed to do, but these couple of weeks have shown us the true precious nature of being in touch often with those we are closest to. Sharing intricate details of our lives and listening for input or maybe just nonjudgmental understanding.

Ava chimed in,

And we also realized, much to our sadness and embarrassment, that we have ignored you and mom as well under the guise of being busy. That you would understand that college kids just don't have the time to check in and be with family. We just wanted to apologize for that and tell you that you and mom are so important to us and that we are committed to not let anything or anyone get in the way of staying in touch with both of you from here on out.

Glenn had sat quietly listening to Ava and Allan. Part of him wanted to shed tears of joy that they "got it". That one of the first customers we all serve are our loved ones. That we serve them with our time, our staying in touch, our listening, our advice, if requested, and, always, our love.

Glenn said with emotion in his voice,

I have always been so proud of both of you but never more so than right now. You've grown into such caring and capable adults—not just because of your educational achievements but also because you have chosen to absorb the values your mom, and, perhaps, a little bit of me have tried to lend to you.

Ava now had tears in her eyes as well and said,

Grandpa, we wanted to talk with you tonight because we have both decided to stay on here with mom for the next few weeks. We are to start our new jobs in a month and so thought we'd take road trips with mom, and she could help us pick out our new homes and help us get settled.

Allan said, "We suspect she would like that a lot as she can still be a 'mom' to us, but also it gives the three of us precious time to talk and enjoy each other."

Ava added, "Grandpa, that means you, Ray and Sergio will be driving home yourselves, and we wanted to make sure you were comfortable with that?"

Glenn jumped in quickly saying,

Absolutely. The three of us will enjoy our time together too so you stay with your mom, make your plans for the next steps in your lives, and just talk and listen. What a precious gift you are giving one another!

You know both of you are interested in service and customer-oriented careers. It's important to bear in mind that communication is really at the heart of all customer service. We have talked so much about several elements that make us good service providers aiming for great, but your ability to realize that if you don't know how to communicate effectively will greatly impact whether your customer service efforts are both well received and appreciated.

Ava and Allan said almost simultaneously, "We knew walking in here with our message that we would learn even more about how to be better. Not just better at customer service but better people. You never disappoint, Grandpa."

Glenn chuckled,

You know me well! At the heart of communication is realizing that there are always at least two (and oftentimes more) people in the conversation. A "sender" of the message and the "receiver." And between my sending you a communication and you receiving it, there is a lot of "noise" that can and very often does serve as a barrier to the message I intended to send being received by you as I planned it.

Ava jumped in,

Wow, Grandpa, that is so true! My boyfriend and I have had to work through times where I would say something sometimes off the top of my head as a thought just jumped in there. He would look at me skeptically wondering where in the world that came from! Occasionally, that would throw us both off, and we would argue about me not listening, him not hearing, and so on.

Allan added,

Yes, as you both know, I can be very spontaneous and that typically means my agenda comes first when I talk with others. I realize now that listening is the key communication skill and that, if my message is important enough, it will still be there when the other person finishes their thought.

Glenn agreed,

So true, both of you. To be a good loved one, friend, and, certainly, successful at work as a customer service excellence provider, we have to subjugate our need to get our message across because we may not even be solving the problem the customer wants addressed until we listen.

We also have to wade through that "noise" I was talking about earlier—things like how many people and messages have they already gotten from our work colleagues before getting to us? That can be very frustrating and confusing. Or do they communicate the same way we do.

Ava said,

I worked part time at several jobs while in school, and, looking back on it, I now realize that I likely used my same word choices, approach, tone of voice, and so on with everyone whether English was their second language or whether they could hear me well. I humbly know now that we all communicate at our own level and that as a good daughter, sister, granddaughter, and customer service provider, I must be watchful for the recipient's needs to make sure my message gets across as I intended.

Allan added,

And that, again, I need to listen to what is said, how it is said, and what isn't said so that I know the right questions to ask in order to serve them well. I need to watch for emotions too. A skill, I will acknowledge, that I have never worked on.

Glenn summarized as a very proud Grandpa,

You both are wonderful people, open to learning and being challenged. You will do well in life but, most importantly, in your personal lives. You both taking the next few weeks with your mom will give her memories that she will treasure forever. Her babies will soon be gone, but she will know that you not only love her but appreciate her wisdom and design hints!

Ava and Allan gave Glenn a kiss on the forehead and a hug as they left his room. Then they headed directly to Liza's room to tell them their plan. To say she was overjoyed is an understatement! As they left her room for the night, Liza sat back and thought what a wonderful several weeks she had had. With her dad and his close friends and her children. It all came together for her. Leaving her current position—one she had fought and worked so very hard for would be the right decision at this stage in her life. Taking those skills and contacts to a not-for-profit organization could bring them to new service heights and would make her feel as if she has so much more to give. This could be an exciting next chapter in her life. Decision made!

Mastering Customer Service

Insight 11: Communication Is the Ultimate Key to Customer Service, and Excellent Listening Skills (With the Ears and Heart) Are the Most Important

The Power of Communication

As Glenn, Ava, and Allan have made clear in this chapter, so much in life is about the ability to communicate clearly, so it's no surprise that communication is equally important in delivering great customer service. Surveys with customers repeatedly show that communication has a huge impact on their satisfaction with a customer experience, and that applies to communication both ways—the customer's ability to get their message across to the service provider and the ability of the service staff to communicate clearly with the customer.

Listen and Understand

Surveys show that customers' ultimate satisfaction with their experience is heavily influenced by what happens at the outset. Do they feel that the person they were dealing with really listened to them and understood what they were requesting? Therefore, all frontline staff who deal directly with customers in retail, hospitality, call centers or any other customer contact roles must start by listening carefully. They must let the customer speak and demonstrate to the customer that they are listening. **When the customer has finished explaining about their problem or making their enquiry, service staff should repeat back their understanding of what the customer has said and what they would like to happen.** It is then essential that they always double-check with the customer *"have I understood you correctly or do you think I have missed anything?"* As Glenn said in this chapter, between the sender of the message and the receiver, there is always a lot of noise, so you can never take it for granted that both parties have the same understanding unless you check. But that's only the first step of the process. Once service providers have ascertained that they have correctly understood the customer's problem or request, they need to communicate back to the customer about what will happen.

Explaining or Providing Information

In many ways, this is a more dangerous area for service providers because they are now in their own field of expertise and explaining things to the customer can become rote because they have done this so many times before. While providing what seems to be simple information to the customer is easy for the service provider, it may well be new and not at all obvious to the customer. Customer service staff could be providing information, advising on product features, explaining what will happen next, or outlining and explaining decisions, for example, the outcome of a complaint. Whatever it is, the rule we highlighted above still applies—always double-check that customers have understood the message and are happy with it. As Ava said in the chapter, *"I worked part time at several jobs while in school, and, looking back on it, I now realize that I likely used my same word choices, approach, tone of voice, and so on with everyone whether English was their second language or whether they could hear me well."* But she had learned that you should never assume that the customer has understood you. Service providers must also understand that, in some cases, customers might be very worried or angry about their situation and so may need significant reassurance or more detailed explanations and plenty of opportunity to ask for clarification or more information. **So the double-check golden rule always applies—***"are you happy with that explanation/the information I have given you, or is there anything else you would like me to explain/any more information you need?"*

Internal Communications

In most organizations, customer-facing staff form a minority of the workforce and rely on receiving good service from other teams if they are to deliver excellent service to external customers. **In organizations that are truly customer-focused all employees will see themselves as delivering services to customers.**[1] The only difference is that some

will be focusing on service to external customers and others on service to internal customers. The importance of this internal chain of great service has been demonstrated empirically. In 1998, in a study by Schneider et al. of 132 bank branches, the score for "interdepartmental service" was the strongest predictor of external customers' perceptions of service quality.[2]

To ensure that the chain of events from operations and support staff to frontline customer service staff is all working toward the same goal of customer satisfaction, it is important to have effective internal communications that make everyone aware of customers' needs and priorities and motivate staff to "think customer" whatever they are doing. As long ago as 1987, Jan Carlzon, CEO of Scandinavian Airlines, was well aware of the importance of internal communications[3] and knew that, to get the message across internally, it's vital to have some simple concepts that staff can relate to. His "moments of truth" catchphrase was perfect. All employees, including those who never have any involvement with external customers, can understand how it feels when they are a customer. They know that, in any customer experience, there are some key moments of truth that are really important and make a huge impact on how they feel about that experience.

While all moments of truth are important, they don't all have the same impact on customer satisfaction. Some moments of truth are what we call Satisfaction Enhancers and others are Satisfaction Maintainers. To explain the difference, we could think of a visit to a restaurant. There are many moments of truth during the restaurant experience, such as the quality of the food, the waiting time to be served, and the cost of the meal. However, two contrasting moments of truth would be the cleanliness of the restaurant and the friendliness of the staff. The cleanliness of the restaurant is a Satisfaction Maintainer. If you walk into a restaurant and it's clearly dirty, it would have such a strong negative impact that you might walk straight back out again without even taking a table. On the other hand, if you walk into a spotlessly clean restaurant you tend to take it for granted. You don't think *Wow, this restaurant is so clean that I'm going to recommend it to all my friends!*" But you would probably tell your friends to avoid the dirty one. The cleanliness of the restaurant is a Satisfaction Maintainer. It is essential to keep the restaurant clean to make sure customers don't have a bad experience that damages your reputation. By contrast, the friendliness of the staff is a Satisfaction Enhancer. As Ava and the three old friends experienced on the way to Liza's holiday home, fantastic, friendly, and attentive staff can make you extremely satisfied and can be the thing you remember most about the experience. The friendliness of the restaurant staff is a Satisfaction Enhancer. Satisfaction Enhancers can make a big impact on customer satisfaction both ways. Unfriendly staff can ruin the experience and make customers very dissatisfied, whereas very friendly staff will make customers satisfied and loyal.

As we have said, **for effective internal communications you need memorable phrases that colleagues will remember.** Shep Hyken[4] developed Jan Carlzon's concept by dividing moments of truth into two types and called them Moments of Magic and Moments of Misery— in other words, Satisfaction Enhancers and Satisfaction Maintainers. **Moments of Misery can only make customers unhappy if they are poor, whereas Moments of Magic can make customers delighted if they are great. What fantastic phrases to make sure all employees understand how much their behavior and attitudes will affect customer satisfaction and, ultimately, the success of the business.**

CHAPTER 12

Coach for Success

Coaching is unlocking people's potential to maximize their own performance. It is helping them to learn rather than teaching them.
—John Whitmore, Author and Coaching Expert

The next morning, Glenn met Ray and Sergio for breakfast and to tell them of the latest travel developments. Glenn explained,

Ava and Allan have decided to spend some precious and personal time with their mom, Liza, as they all are entering a new phase of their lives. They credit the three of us for helping them see not only a variety of new concepts regarding what customer service really is but how it starts at home. Both kids want to remain here with Liza for the rest of the summer—just like they used to as small children. They want to support her in a huge career move and just enjoy one another as adults.

"Wow!" Ray said.

It looks like we still have something to give even when we have retired and moved out of most or all of our official roles. I have so enjoyed being with you both this summer, and getting to know Liza, Ava, and Allan has been a pleasure. To know that we actually impacted them personally as well as professionally is the cherry on top of the sundae!

Sergio offered,

I've been a firm believer for a very long time that we always have more to give—we just need to find the opportunities and act on them. Coaching is such a natural offshoot of our careers and personal lives. Perhaps our new purpose is to help others grow in their knowledge and application of service excellence through the experiences of people like us who have "been there" and who embrace the notion of service excellence as one of the greatest of impacts on society.

Glenn agreed,

There is a true need to build a cadre of service excellence enthusiasts across businesses. People should realize that passion about service excellence begets service excellence. Everyone benefits—customers, employees, stakeholders. Making service excellence a way of life trickles out from a business into everyone's personal and community life.

Sergio shared,

As executives in our own businesses, we tried to be role models for service excellence, hoping it would transform our organizations and the world to some extent. Excellent service elevates satisfaction and increases joy and happiness, hopefully, snowballing to all of society. Service excellence can lead to so much positivity and can change the world. One service excellence experience at a time! I know it sounds like a pipedream and too large to ever achieve, but I'm game for continuing to push those within my influence in that direction.

Glenn and Ray said with emotion, "We're in!"
Sergio looked at his watch and suggested,

We'd better finish packing and then load the car to begin the drive home, but I wondered what you both thought about taking our time on the return trip. Stopping at out-of-the-way overnight places and small diners to experience more of the wonders of our country and its people on the way home.

Ray and Glenn once again said with laughter, "We're in!"

A few hours later the car was loaded and Liza, Ava, and Allan were standing with Ray, Sergio, and Glenn to say their goodbyes. Liza had tears in her eyes as she said,

I have so enjoyed having you all with us for the past few weeks. Thank you for deciding to spend your precious time with us and for all of the sharing you offered us. I have grown so much this summer, and it is all due to the three of you.

Allan and Ava gave the men a hug. Ava smiled and said,

Grandpa, we totally agree with mom. The three of you taught us a lot and helped us grow. Allan and I have talked a lot about your thoughts on life, in general, but service excellence specifically. We both feel like we have a solid hold on what we can, should, and must do when we start our new jobs this fall. We only wish everyone could have this crash course in the realities of customer service and how to build on those opportunities.

"I totally agree," said Allan.

I came here this summer to have a good time, rest, fish, enjoy grandpa, you Ava, mom, and grandpa's friends. Never did I think I would walk away with so much practical knowledge and develop new friendships. Your guidance on our careers and how to start them out will be invaluable, but sticking with the highest of standards for customer service will put us at a level of influence with our peers. Through your help, we are now in a position to elevate service excellence in our future workplaces. We very much appreciate all your help and advice!

Liza reminded them, "We're going on that European tour next summer! After we all get home and for the three of us, settled in our new jobs, let's start the planning."

Glenn hugged Liza, Ava, and Allan saying,

Yes, Europe is on, but I look forward to talking with all of you over video conferencing frequently so that I can stay up-to-date on your lives. Thank you for your hospitality, and please know you taught us a lot too.

Ray and Sergio said their goodbyes and thanks, and the three gentlemen were off on the trip home.

After a quiet hour on the road, Ray said,

You know, I've been thinking more about what we were discussing earlier—offering coaching on customer service to whomever might be interested. It could be an interesting venture to pursue at this stage in our lives. We can continue making an impact on the lives of others.

Glenn said, "I was thinking about the exact same thing only I am hoping we can figure out how we can also reach those that don't know they need coaching as well!"

As a military officer, I've learned that a coach is anyone who teaches, trains, or directs another. This person could be a supervisor, colleague, customer, or someone on the street. There are countless opportunities to coach others and learn from them as well. Coaching could be a way to spread and enhance the practice of service excellence. We can certainly do this for companies or individuals. We don't have to do too much of it. We could do a project here or there and pursue those cases where we can really make a difference.

The men sat quietly while giving the matter some thought.

Glenn asked whether they were ready to stop for a bite of lunch, and all three agreed that the next small diner they came to would be the spot.

A short while later, they saw signs for the Redbird Diner and pulled in. Ray commented, "It looks a little 'sketchy' but let's give it a try." All agreed and in they went.

They were greeted by a smiling wait staff member who had a smear of ketchup on her uniform and was carrying the largest tray full of food any of them had ever seen.

Ray smiled back at "Sally" and asked for a table for three. She pointed them in a direction toward the back of the diner and said, "Help yourself to any open table. Restrooms are through the doors that way, and I'll be right with you in five minutes."

The three selected a table and sat down. Sergio commented, "Her smile was so welcoming, but I'm curious about stating in absolute minutes when she would be back to wait on us. That sounded so firm as if she was setting an expectation for herself as well as us."

Glenn agreed,

You know, as a "coach," I would suggest to her that there might be things out of her control that wouldn't allow her to be back to us in five minutes, and so an expectation set may not be able to be met.

"While I appreciate the intention, I agree with you, Glenn," Ray said. "Maybe our 'coaching' to her should be acknowledgment of the effort and intent but that she should always "make the promises she can keep and keep the promises she makes."

Sally had come up to them and overheard the last sentence. She said,

Hi guys, couldn't help but overhear your conversation. You seem like fine gentlemen, perhaps I can explain where I am coming from. I always set a time goal for myself with each interaction so that I keep myself motivated to aim for service excellence. I know that probably seems silly to you all because all I'm doing is serving food, but it's important to me to do a good job in everything I do. There isn't much in my control at this point in my life, so I try to find things that are in my control and capitalize on those.

Ray blushed with some embarrassment.

Sally, you are absolutely right. If something is worth doing with your time, it should be done the best possible way. You have figured out a viable approach toward excellent service with your timeframe method. Kudos to you! It works differently for different people. You remind me that it is so easy to give advice without knowing much about the overall circumstances. and the advice could be ironically on target or way off base.

Glenn shrugged saying,

Sally, you have taught three old guys a valuable lesson today about offering input when it isn't requested even when you feel like you have a pretty good picture of the entire issue at hand. Even at our age, we still have a lot to learn. We hope we didn't offend you.

Sally smiled, "No, no … not at all. I thought it would be best to clarify my actions so that you wouldn't think I'm being rude or insensitive."
Sergio agreed.

Sally, we are glad that you explained the matter to us. It gave us a new insight to think about. We learned from your feedback. When anyone thinks they have "arrived" and pretty much have all of the knowledge they need, they are painfully wrong and foolish. You have reminded us that, while we may have a lot to offer others with our long careers and expertise, we still have a lot to learn as well. Thank you for giving us a good lesson today.

Sally smiled, "You're welcome. Now, what can I get you for lunch today?"
The men smiled back and mentioned their choices.
Later, as they were on the road again, Ray said, "That episode with Sally was humbling."

Yes, it was. You know the role of a coach depending on the issue at play is to be a motivator, an evaluator, a developer, a mediator, or a disciplinarian—or maybe all five of those!

said Glenn. "Sally sure motivated me after she served as a mediator in our conversation and evaluated its intent from her perspective. She helped me develop a different take on her actions and not to prejudge with limited information."

Ray added tongue-in-cheek, "And I felt a bit disciplined too, although she did it in a very tactful and cordial manner."

It was nearing time to stop for dinner and an overnight stay, so they started looking for potential food and sleeping options. They passed several that didn't seem to meet their unspoken expectations until they saw a Bed and Breakfast (B&B) that looked welcoming. They pulled in and Ray went inside to see if they had rooms for the night.

He came out quickly and waved his fellow travelers in. "It's not fancy but clean, and the person at the desk was very pleasant. Should we give it a try?"

Glenn and Sergio said simultaneously, "Sure" and they all went in with their overnight bags.

They were greeted by an elderly gentleman at the front desk who didn't rise from his chair but smiled at them and got them registered for three adjoining rooms on the main floor. The B&B didn't have an elevator, and so he mentioned to the three men that he put them on the main floor to avoid stairs.

The men had moved into their respective rooms, and a few moments later reconvened in the far end portion of the lobby. Glenn quietly commented that, while he knew he looked "old," he didn't like to be treated as if he were "old."

Sergio responded, "Yes, initially, I felt that way too but decided to assume that Charlie at the front desk was just being thoughtful. Perhaps he is a 'coaching' opportunity for us to discuss?"

"Well," Ray said, "Having learned a lesson from being overheard by Sally, discussing how we would coach Charlie should be done behind closed doors. Let's proceed to my room. I have a small bottle of whiskey there."

When the men got to the room, Ray poured whiskey in the glasses and passed them around.

He took a sip of the whiskey and said, "We need to refine our coaching approach to others, especially when advice is not requested."

OK, so I would say that one of us could share with Charlie that we felt a little put off about our ages being an issue on assigning the rooms for us. That perhaps the better approach might have been to ask if we preferred an upper level room with a better view and a deck, realizing there is no elevator and no bell staff to assist with luggage or a first-floor room where we have a patio out to the garden and no stairs, said Sergio.

Glenn shared,

Yes, three of us talking with him could feel like an 'attack' even though that isn't our intention. Plus sharing our thoughts in a quiet more private setting seems less intimidating and more a consideration for the future than a complaint.

Ray offered to find the opportunity to talk with Charlie representing only himself and not bringing the thoughts of Glenn and Sergio into the conversation as, again, that can feel very intimidating.

Later, Ray shared with the other two, "Shortly after dinner—which was excellent, wasn't it—Charlie was at the linen closet straightening some things out, and no one else was around, so I took just a minute to share with him my thoughts on room assignments."

He took it very well and said that he was probably thinking more about his own physical challenges. He apologized for any inference that we all weren't capable of making it to the upper floors, and I assured him that no apology was necessary. That we just wanted him to keep getting better and better, and perhaps this small suggestion would assist with that.

Sergio asked, "How did he seem at the end of the conversation?"

Ray responded, "He was definitely fine, and we proceeded to talk about our kids and grandkids, how lovely the B&B and its restaurant are. I also mentioned how pleasant and efficient he was in registering us."

Glenn said,

I'm not a fan of the "sandwich" approach where you compliment someone, hit them with the opportunity to improve, and close with a compliment. It always feels like I am downplaying both the importance of the need to improve and the sincerity of the compliment. How do you all feel about that?

Ray nodded,

I agree, Glenn, and so I avoid doing that as well. With Charlie, since we likely will not be a recipient of his services ever again, I thought leaving him with a compliment would work well for this time. He can choose to take or leave my coaching advice on the assessment of a customer's needs based on apparent age.

"Speaking of age. I think at our age, it's about bedtime" said Sergio. Ray and Glenn laughed.

The next morning on the road again, they started talking about the qualities of successful coaches. Ray said,

I am getting excited about this new venture we're considering. The three of us are in a position to coach people as well as companies and help them improve performance in the customer service arena. Last night I got to thinking about what the qualities of successful coaches are.

Sergio offered,

I taught a few classes over the years on coaching and here are some of the qualities I feel are needed to be a successful coach.

First of all, you have to really like coaching because you have no control over whether those you are working with will embrace your suggestions or not. Doing your best and then letting go can be a challenge. As a professor, I faced that thousands of times over the years—I'm pretty good at letting go! And you must be committed to the process as, most often this isn't a "one and done" event.

"You know, another required quality from my perspective for a successful coach is maintaining confidentiality. That really fits in the wheelhouse for each of us, given our careers" Glenn offered. "Also, a coach has to be an excellent listener—with the ears, the eyes, the brain, and the heart—and know how and when to provide feedback."

"I agree," said Ray.

Being sensitive to the needs of others is critical in a coaching role. Timing of the advice matters as well. It isn't about the coach per se but, rather, the needs of the person being coached. A good coach must also be well organized, as the coaching process is a building-block type of setup, and the coach has to always have the next step ready to go.

Glenn reminded the three men,

Sergio, back to your earlier point, a good coach must relinquish dominance and control depending on the purpose of the coaching intervention as that can affect the potential for positive outcomes. That can be difficult for established leaders.

The three men were quiet in the car for a good deal of the trip home, reflecting on the past few weeks, the future trip to Europe, and their planned new coaching venture. When they arrived home, they hugged each other with a new sincerity appreciating the level of their relationship as it had grown recently.

Glenn said with some emotion,

I am so glad you both came on this trip and that we realized how important old friends are to each of us. I'm looking forward to working with you all. We were a team in the earlier part of our lives. We pursued different paths and have now reunited in our twilight years to pursue our mutual dream of making a difference in the world. We can share what we learned in our careers and continue to build on a passion we shared even during our high school days—service excellence.

"Well said, Glenn. Let's set a video conference two weeks from now so that we don't get pulled back into our old lives and forget the importance of this special relationship and how we want to share our skills with others on a limited and yet meaningful basis." Sergio said.

Ray offered, "Let's compare calendars right now and set the date for our next get-together! We can share updates from each of our families and then concentrate on our coaching venture. I feel like I have a whole new purpose!"

The three set a date for their video conference, and Sergio offered to draft the initial talk points for the meeting so that they remained focused. With hugs and a few tears, the three went their own ways more excited about their future than they had ever imagined!

Mastering Customer Service

Insight 12: Coaching Is a Universal Tool for Teaching, Training and Directing

Everyone Can Be a Coach

Coaching is teaching, training, and directing. We often think of the Supervisor in the workplace being the coach, and the person being coached is the Supervisor's direct report. But to fully benefit from coaching, we must expand this view to think of a coach as anyone who teaches, trains, or directs another person in any situation **regardless of title/authority**. Could any employee "coach" a colleague or a supervisor? Absolutely. **All of the available knowledge and experience aren't resident in only those with a title of authority**.

This chapter offers several reminders about how many coaching opportunities we have in life both to take advantage of for ourselves personally and to offer to others. Ray, Glenn, and Sergio tell us that **we all always have more to give—we just need to find the opportunities and act on them.**

Regardless of where we are in our careers, education, or lives, coaching is a natural offshoot. For those that are retired from their jobs, perhaps the new purpose is to help others grow in their knowledge and application of service excellence through the experiences of people who have "been there" and who embrace the notion of service excellence as one of the greatest of impacts on society.

Sergio encourages us all to remain **role models** as we interact in the world of service. That responsibility doesn't end with leaving a job or company or career. In fact, it is, perhaps, even more important to relay service excellence needs and opportunities as we impress on others not just our life experience but also our expectations as a customer.

Glenn reminds us that, oftentimes, people don't realize that they could use some coaching, so **having a good relationship** with co-workers and those you may supervise pays off, particularly when a coaching opportunity arises.

And not all coaching is spur of the moment. **Momentary mentoring/coaching is unplanned and capitalizes on the numerous**

opportunities daily to lend insight into a colleague or a direct report on how something might be better/alternatively done. Again, **the status of the relationship leading into that coaching experience will decide how well the input is accepted and used.**

Glenn also counsels us that **coaching can happen with a customer, a colleague, a supervisor, a fellow volunteer—anyone with whom you are interacting and pursuing a like goal.** With the right intention and even on the spur of the moment, coaching can be a wonderful tool to broaden perspective and improve the circumstance now and down the road.

As we appreciate what each of us has to lend to others and that we still have growth opportunities ourselves, there are **three points within this chapter which deserve special consideration.**

What Are the Roles of Coaching?

Too often, in the past, "coaching" had a negative connotation being tied to poor employee performance. It also tended to be more reactive in nature and may well have contributed to adversarial relationships between the "coach" and the person being coached. Fortunately, we are **evolving into a more positive view of the role of a coach—more proactive in identifying new prospects for growth and challenges in persuading people to consider an alternative approach.** Coaching **absolutely requires a respectful relationship with the person being coached to better assure a positive outcome.**

The **standard coaching roles include:**

- **Evaluator**: Appraises performance formally (in a performance evaluation) or informally (as opportunities/needs arise). There is an element of authority in this role.
- **Motivator**: Emphasizes or confirms expectations from rewards/ recognition to punitive actions. Authority may be present in this role as well, but we all should find opportunities to motivate those around us and with whom we share like goals.

- **Developer**: works with someone on activities like setting/monitoring/supporting personal goals. Again, authority may be a part of this role but we can all help support others' goals especially if they are shared.
- **Mediator**: Identifies the root cause of a (work) relationship breakdown and brings affected parties together to seek a mutually acceptable resolution. This likely requires authority, but, very often, mediators are third parties who know the mediation process but remain objective to the discussion and outcomes.
- **Disciplinarian**: When other mechanisms haven't worked, the coach/supervisor identifies specific opportunities/requirements for improvement with associated expectations and the benefits of compliance/consequences of noncompliance.[1] This is an authoritative role.

Effective coaches play a variety of roles, but not every coach performs all roles. **Find the roles you can and should play. Each of us can, at the least, motivate and help develop others**. That should and must be part of our goals in interacting with others.

What Are the Qualities of Successful Coaches?

While the bulk of coaching likely comes from Leadership, we all should challenge ourselves to develop certain **characteristics that allow us to be good coaches:**

1. A belief in empowerment and the embodiment of that concept in every interaction. **Empowerment can be defined as: the granting of the power, right, or authority to perform various acts or duties**. Instilling into people a deep sense of ownership and accountability is the precursor of successful empowerment. Employees who are empowered willingly take accountability for their actions and seek greater opportunities to grow and serve. Part of empowerment is everyone celebrating the

accomplishments of their colleagues. **Fear, insecurity, jealousy, and competition have no place in successful businesses, and empowered employees have no need for those feelings because they know how invaluable their services and positive attitude are to the employer.**[2]

2. Commitment to the growth of the people whom we are mentoring. We should **"nurture talent" by finding opportunities for mentees to learn, grow, share, and celebrate their new-found knowledge.** We show value for those those we are coaching by lending our time (even when it isn't convenient) and expertise along with access to opportunities to grow. **Coaches readily acknowledge that it isn't about them but about the people they have the privilege of coaching. The time to shine is for the mentee—never the mentor/coach.** Good coaches reflect in real-time support for **continuous improvement.**[2]

3. Excellent listeners (with the eyes, ears, and heart). When a **trusting relationship is developed**, the mentee is typically more willing to accept input and apply it from their coach which leads to a trusting relationship focused on having felt 'heard'. **Constructive feedback is willingly received and even sought** because the mentee knows that the coach has their best interests at heart. As a good communicator, the **coach is the role model for providing timely, specific, and goal-supporting input** on methods and behaviors. That means the coach, when possible, has planned out the conversation ahead of time for everyone's benefit. **While many coaching opportunities are spontaneous, knowing basically where the mentee is on their goals and what the general next step in achieving those goals may be allows the coach to always be as prepared as possible.** Good coaches **listen more than they speak.** Helping the mentee come up with the next step after agreeing on a solution for the step under discussion is teaching the mentee how to think like that on their own. **Dialogue driven by trust is the successful measure of a great coach.**[2]

4. Our business world is very competitive, and the only difference between your like business and that of the one down the street is your people. **Being flexible in processes and approaches, promoting continuous learning and using those outcomes, and embracing change in its truest form not only allow your organization (and you) to evolve** but promote both as leaders in your field. Be adaptable, especially with your own role showing by example that you are also a **change artist.**[2]

Curiosity, courage, and compassion drive an exceptional coach[3], and **resilience, adaptability, and empathy are the key elements** of a successful coach and, therefore, successful employees and a thriving organization.[2] And being sensitive to the mentee with the **timing of the coaching, words used, expectations set forth, and assuring confidentiality leads to a working relationship filled with respect and likely success.**

And always remember that despite your years of experience, your education, and your title/responsibilities—you don't know it all! Part of relationship building is not making assumptions about the needed coaching without doing a little "digging" first.

Perhaps most importantly—excellent **coaches make the promises they can keep and keep the promises they make!**[4]

What Are the Coaching Steps That Will Lead to a Successful Engagement?

While coaching steps vary by the situation, **successful outcomes typically implement the following steps:**

1. The **coach and the mentee both agree** that an opportunity exists for the latter to grow, improve, and learn as part of performance empowerment. With **no alignment of purpose, the engagement will likely be futile.**

2. Both parties agree to an **open mind** and what that means in this engagement, especially as it relates to alternative solutions for the growth opportunity at hand.

3. Both parties agree on the **ultimate/high-level goals of the engagement and identify first steps/responsible parties/timelines.**

4. **A follow-up schedule is set with both parties responsible for meeting their duties within the engagement. Both people "own" the successful outcomes.**

5. The **coach recognizes and acknowledges all improvements—** small and large as well as providing constructive feedback as warranted all to assure that the ultimate/sought-after goals are achieved.[1]

The coach and the mentee must also **commit to the time it will likely take to achieve the goals** through the coaching process. It is rarely a "one and done" event. **Coaches must also be good at comfortably stepping back** and letting the mentee go through some trial and error in order to learn. The coach being the mentee's backup and invisible support is critical to the mentee feeling comfortable in venturing out on their own.

People feel valued when they are given the opportunity to grow and learn functionally and attitudinally, and coaching provides that vehicle. The best coaches have the privilege of **enhancing the self-esteem of those they coach whether it is a planned engagement with one's supervisor or a momentary mentoring opportunity where the relationship is built literally at that moment.**

At the heart of coaching is the willingness to invest in others with everyone winning. We need to **use everyone's skills, education, training, and experience to gain and retain the best advantage** over our competitors and to provide opportunities to each employee to lend their expertise in all kinds of ways which benefits them and the company.[1]

Epilogue

This featured story highlights what we call the **Customer Service Dozen**—12 key approaches essential for achieving excellence in careers anchored on customer service:

Insight 1: Help Others
Insight 2: Take Time to Understand
Insight 3: "Live" the Mission
Insight 4: Identify and Deliver a Consistent High-Value Proposition
Insight 5: Seek and Use Feedback
Insight 6: Reinvent Yourself Constantly
Insight 7: Collaborate While Maintaining Ownership
Insight 8: Make the Ultimate Investment
Insight 9: Motivate and Empower
Insight 10: Make Every Interaction Positive
Insight 11: Leverage Communication
Insight 12: Coach for Success

When implementing the **Customer Service Dozen**, attention needs to be placed across three levels: Self, Others, and Environment.

In the quest for customer service excellence, we need to manage ourselves and take proactive action in assisting others. Strategies relating to Self include the following: Take Time to Understand, "Live" the Mission, Identify and Deliver a High-Value Proposition, Reinvent Yourself Constantly, and Make Every Interaction Positive. **It is only when we truly understand our own intentions and take steps that are well aligned with who we are and what we're about, will we be able to deliver consistently meaningful and impactful service.**

Thinking about others is the hallmark of real customer service.
The **strategies relating to Others are as follows:** Help Others,
Collaborate While Maintaining Ownership, Make the Ultimate
Investment, Motivate and Empower, Leverage Communication,
and Coach for Success. **When serving others, a giving spirit
along with an empathetic and collaborative nature provides
the framework for the identification of real needs and the provision of real solutions.**

**Knowing the environment sets the stage for effective customer
service implementation. An important strategy is to Seek
and Use Feedback.** Understanding the operational terrain well,
including challenges, opportunities, and best practices, will help
in effective planning and execution. It is important to remember
that **customer service excellence is never a one-shot proposition, it takes time and requires several iterations to get to an
optimal level.**

The effective execution of the 12 strategies within one's **Self**, toward
Others, and across the right **Environment** leads to consistent customer
service excellence.

In customer service careers, knowledge of **Self**, genuine concern for
Others, and a keen understanding of the workplace **Environment** will
result in noticeable and noteworthy accomplishments.

In customer service, parallelisms exist. For example, companies often
define themselves by their mission and culture. This organizational perception often defines the priorities they make and the actions they take.
A company may **embrace a philosophy of "Customer First," meaning
the highest level of attention has to be placed on the needs of the
customer at all times**. Building on this philosophy, they would likely
end up creating policies and organizational structures that would lead to
the consistent provision of the highest level of customer care. In essence,
**what they believe in and imagine themselves to be becomes a fulfilling
prophecy.**

There are many companies looking to enhance their service quality, and each of us can draw from the insights featured in this story to accomplish ongoing and amazing customer service with every interaction. In addition, knowing others (i.e., the customers) and the environment (i.e., competition, industry, market, and economy) well puts the company in a good position to create effective strategies that raise the bar and change the game of customer service.

It is not uncommon today for companies to use artificial intelligence to know their customers better, engage them more, customize service offerings, predict sales, and even capture and respond to emerging trends quickly. Many companies are proactively managing their social media accounts to gain a competitive edge. Others diligently explore ways to get more five-star service ratings from customers. **Pursuing a service strategy that converges organizational understanding of Self, Others, and Environment puts a company on a path toward consistent customer service excellence.**

The **cohesive connectedness and alignment of the three strategic levels lead to success. The absence of any single element could result in poor implementation and even failure.**

Service careers and corporate customer service need to be well planned out. Meticulous planning can make all the difference. Companies with exceptional customer service did not get to and stay at that level by chance. Their customer service model was planned and implemented with ample talent, support, and financial resources.

Embracing a service-oriented attitude and mindset on an individual and organizational level is important. For instance, **attributes such as empathy, flexibility, excellent listening, effective communication, and the spirit and determination to serve make a huge difference in achieving and maintaining superior customer service.**

A well-prepared Customer Service Strategic Plan is recommended for companies of all sizes. This plan needs to cover all the essentials for the delivery of outstanding customer service, including required talent, research, technology, operational support, and financial resources. In a growingly competitive, information-driven digital age where a five-star service rating is the ultimate badge of honor, companies need to continually find new ways to define themselves and create amazing customer experiences.

The attainment of customer service excellence in careers is not easy. Countless obstacles exist, competition intensifies, and the bar seems to keep getting higher. **Victory, however, belongs not necessarily to those with the most talent or resources but rather those who know who and where they are and possess a deep desire to provide exceptional service for all.**

References

Chapter 1

1. Adam Smith. 1776. "The Wealth of Nations."
2. Claes Fornell et al. 2005. *The American Customer Satisfaction Index at Ten Years: Implications for the Economy, Stock Returns and Management*, Stephen M Ross School of Business, University of Michigan.
3. Heskett, Sasser and Schlesinger. 2003. *The Value-Profit Chain*, Free Press, New York.
4. Leon Festinger. 1957. *A Theory of Cognitive Dissonance*, Stanford University Press, Stanford.
5. Frederick Reichheld. 2001. *The Loyalty Effect*, 2nd edition, Harvard Business School Press, Boston.
6. Sasser and Jones. 1995. *Why Satisfied Customers Defect*, Harvard Business Review, November-December.
7. Rust, Zahorik and Keiningham. 1996. *Making Service Quality Financially Accountable*, in "Readings in Service Marketing", Harper Collins.
8. "Experience is everything: Here's how to get it right", PwC: https://www.pwc.com/us/en/services/consulting/library/consumer-intelligence-series/future-of-customer-experience.html.
9. Heskett, Sasser and Schlesinger. 1997. *The Service-Profit Chain*, Free Press, New York.

Chapter 2

1. Kotler, P. 1986. *Marketing Management: Analysis, Planning and Control*, Prentice-Hall International, Englewood Cliffs, New Jersey.
2. Johnson and Gustafsson. 2000. "Improving Customer Satisfaction, Loyalty and Profit: An Integrated Measurement and Management System." John Wiley and Sons, San Francisco, California.
3. Hill, Roche and Allen. 2007. *Customer Satisfaction: The Customer Experience Through the Customer's Eyes*. Cogent Publishing, England.

Chapter 3

1. Babcock, J. 2023. "Why Your Company Needs a Mission Statement + Examples and Tips." info@www.leaders.com.
2. Dukes, A., and Y. Zhu. May–June 2019. "Why Customer Service Frustrates Consumers: Using a Tiered Organizational Structure to Exploit Hassle Costs," *Informs, Marketing Science* 38 (3).
3. Kappel, M. 2022. "Contributor, Is Customer Service Still Important? On a Scale of 1 To 10, It's an 11." *Forbes Small Business Strategy.* www.forbes.com/sites/mikekappel/2022/07/20/is-customer-service-still-important-on-a-scale-of-1-to-10-its-an-11/?sh=483b51a14f85.
4. Leung, F.F., K. Sara and C.H. Tse. 2020. "Highlighting Effort Versus Talent in Service Employee Performance: Customer Attributions and Responses." *American Marketing Association, Journal of Marketing* 84 (3).
5. Crutcher, C.W. 2017. *Managing Service Excellence.* National Customer Service Association.

Chapter 4

1. Crutcher, C.W. 2017. *Managing Service Excellence.* National Customer Service Association.
2. Dixon, M., K. Freeman, and N. Toman. 2010. "Stop Trying to Delight Your Customers." *Harvard Business Review.*
3. Hinds, R. and S. Gupta. 2023. "Customer Experience Is Everyone's Responsibility." *Harvard Business Review.*
4. Iwuozor, J. 2024. "What Is Customer Service? Definition & Best Practices." *Forbes Media.*

Chapter 5

1. Hays, S. 1970. *An Outline of Statistics.* Longman, London.
2. Kish, L. 1965. *Survey Sampling.* New York, NY: John Wiley & Sons.
3. Hill, Roche, and Allen. 2007. *Customer Satisfaction: The Customer Experience Through the Customer's Eyes.* Cogent Publishing, England.
4. American Customer Satisfaction Index (ACSI).
5. United Kingdom Customer Satisfaction Index (UKCSI).
6. Keiningham, Vavra, Aksoy, and Wallard. 2005. *Loyalty Myths.* New Jersey: John Wiley & Sons, Hoboken.
7. Myers, J.H. 1999. *Measuring Customer Satisfaction: Hot Buttons and Other Measurement Issues.* American Marketing Association, Chicago.

8. Szwarc, P. 2005. *Researching Customer Satisfaction and Loyalty.* Kogan Page, London.

9. Morrison, Colman, and Preston. 1997. "Mystery Customer Research: Cognitive Processes Affecting Accuracy." *Journal of the Market Research Society* 46 (4).

10. Heskett, Sasser, and Schlesinger. 1997. *The Service-Profit Chain.* New York, NY: Free Press.

Chapter 6

1. Smith, M. 2024. "107 Customer Service Statistics and Facts You Shouldn't Ignore." Help Scout.

2. Amaresan, S. 2023. "Why Customer Service is Important: 16 Data-Backed Facts to Know." HubSpot, Inc.

3. Crutcher, C.W. 2017. *Managing Service Excellence.* National Customer Service Association,

Chapter 7

1. Luft, J., and H. Ingram. 1955. "Health Education England." *Johari Window.* www.hee.nhs.uk.files.Johariwindow.

2. Crutcher, C.W. 2017. *Managing Service Excellence.* National Customer Service Association.

Chapter 8

1. Smith, M. 2024. "107 Customer Service Statistics and Facts You Shouldn't Ignore." *Help Scout/Hub Spot/Khoros/Salesforce Research/McKinsey/KPMG.*

2. Super Office AS (HQ). n.d. "How to Deliver Great Customer Service (With 5 Real Examples." Accessed 2024.

3. Gunarathne, P., H. Rui, and A. Seidmann. 2018. "When Social Media Delivers Customer Service: Differential Customer Treatment in the Airline Industry." *MIS Quarterly* 42 (2). www.misq.org.

4. Crutcher, C.W. 2017. *Managing Service Excellence.* National Customer Service Association.

5. Dixon, M., K. Freeman, and N. Toman. 2010. "Stop Trying to Delight Your Customers." *Harvard Business Review.*

Chapter 9

1. Heskett, Sasser, and Schlesinger.1997. *The Service Profit Chain*, New York, NY: Free Press.

2. Lowenstein, M. 2015. "Creeping Meatballism at Work: How BofA Dismantled MBNA's Customer-Centric Culture." *Customer Think*, December.

3. Heskett, Sasser, and Schlesinger. 2003. *The Value Profit Chain*. Free Press, New York.

4. Mogelonsky, L., and A. Mogelonsky. August 2023. "Measuring the Customer Lifetime Value of Hotel Guests." *Hotel News Now.*

5. Sewell, C., and P.B. Brown. 1998. *Customers for Life*. New York, NY: Pocket Books.

Chapter 10

1. Super Office AS (HQ). n.d. "How to Deliver Great Customer Service (With 5 Real Examples)." Accessed 2024.

2. Page, M. 2024. michaelpage.com.au

3. Covey, S.R. 1989. "The Seven Habits of Highly Effective People." *Franklin-Covey.* www.franklincovey.com.

4. Bouchard, J. 2015. "Four Keys of Efficiency and Effectiveness." *Johanne Bouchard.* www.johannebouchard.com.

Chapter 11

1. Barwise and Meehan. 2004. *Simply Better: Winning and Keeping Customers By Delivering What Matters Most*. Boston: Harvard Business School Press.

2. Schneider, White, and Paul. 1998. "Linking Service Climate and Customer Perceptions of Service Quality: Test of a Causal Model." *Journal of Applied Psychology* 83 (2).

3. Carlzon, J. 1987. *Moments of Truth: New Strategies for Today's Customer-Driven Economy*. Cambridge, Mass: Ballinger Publishing Company.

4. Hyken, S. 1993. *Moments of Magic: Be a Star With Your Customers & Keep Them Forever*. Saint Louis, MO: Alan Press.

Chapter 12

1. Crutcher, C.W. 2017. *Managing Service Excellence*. National Customer Service Association.

2. Dennison, K. 2023. "What Is a Coaching Leadership Style." *University of Phoenix.*

3. T. Rowe Price. 2020. "Understanding the "3C's" of Coaching. 2020, Next Wave of Wealth Research."

4. Covey, S.R. 1989. "The Seven Habits of Highly Effective People." Franklin Covey. www.franklincovey.com.

About the Authors

J. Mark Munoz is a tenured Full Professor of Management and International Business at Millikin University in Illinois. He was a former Visiting Fellow at the Kennedy School of Government at Harvard University. He is a recipient of several awards, including four Best Research Paper Awards, a Literary Award, two International Book Awards, the Accreditation Council for Business Schools and Programs Teaching Excellence Award, among others. He was recognized by the Academy of Global Business Advancement (AGBA) as the 2016 Distinguished Business Dean and recognized for Global Academic Excellence by Amity/IEEE in 2019. In 2024, he received AGBA's Lifetime Achievement Award in Global Business. Aside from top-tier journal publications, he has authored/edited/coedited over 25 books, including *International Social Entrepreneurship, Handbook on the Geopolitics of Business, Global Business Intelligence, Arts and Entrepreneurship, Managerial Forensics, Creating a Business and Personal Legacy, The Next Right Move, The AI Leader*, and *Digital Entrepreneurship and the Global Economy*. He directs consulting projects worldwide in the areas of strategy formulation, international sales and marketing, and international finance and business development.

Nigel Hill is the founder of TLF Research Ltd, a UK company that has been a leader in customer satisfaction for 30 years. TLF provides research services, advice, design and communications services, and training to help organizations measure, monitor, and improve their customers' experience. Nigel has written four books about customer satisfaction, including *Customer Satisfaction: The Customer Experience Through the Customers' Eyes, The Handbook of Customer Satisfaction Measurement, How to Measure Customer Satisfaction*, and *Customer Satisfaction for ISO 9000*. He has also written many articles on the subject and has spoken on the subject at conferences and events around the world. Nigel holds a BSc (Econ) from the London School of Economics, a Master of Philosophy from the University of Huddersfield, and a Diploma in Marketing.

Diane M. Crutcher is the Vice President of Programs for the National Customer Service Association (U.S.). Ms. Crutcher has significant experience in leading teams and projects, human resource development, and in continuous quality improvement process design and implementation. Her extremely high skill sets in the area of human dynamics allow her to guide and direct individuals and groups in the provision of Service Excellence. Ms. Crutcher is well-regarded for her ability to work with individuals and groups in effective problem solving. She holds a large number of business certifications, including Certified Continuous Quality Improvement facilitator, "LEAN" Process facilitator, Certified Teams Assessor, "The 7 Habits of Highly Effective People" Master facilitator, Diversity trainer, a Work Complexity Analyst, Certified Leading Empowered Organizations facilitator, and a Certified Principle-Centered Leadership facilitator. Ms. Crutcher is highly recognized for her ability to "lead the way forward" for individuals and groups—even in the most challenging of circumstances. She has been an adult educator for over 20 years and holds a bachelor's degree in Psychology and a master's degree in Education both from Illinois State University. Her career has been in leadership positions in finance and a national not-for-profit organization as well as serving as a Human Resources Director in the health care arena.

Index

www.ingramcontent.com/pod-product-compliance
Lightning Source LLC
Chambersburg PA
CBHW061312220326
41599CB00026B/4842